PROPHETS, PIONEERS AND POSSIBILITIES

Sermons for Pentecost (Last Third)
Cycle C First Lesson Texts

BY RICHARD A. HASLER

C.S.S Publishing Co., Inc.
Lima, Ohio

PROPHETS, PIONEERS AND POSSIBILITIES

Copyright © 1991 by
The C.S.S. Publishing Company, Inc.
Lima, Ohio

All rights reserved. No part of this publication may be reproduced, stored in a retrieval system, or transmitted in any form or by any means, electronic, mechanical, photocopying, recording, or otherwise, without the prior permission of the publisher. Inquiries should be addressed to: The C.S.S. Publishing Company, Inc., 628 South Main Street, Lima, Ohio 45804.

Library of Congress Cataloging-in-Publication Data
Hasler, Richard A.
  Prophets, pioneers and possibilities : sermons for Pentecost (last third) : cycle C first lesson texts / by Richard A. Hasler.
      p.   cm.
  ISBN 1-55673-321-6
  1. Pentecost season — Sermons.   2. Sermons, American.   I. Title.
BV4300.5H37   1991
252'.6—dc20
                                                                91-17599
                                                                     CIP

9142 / ISBN 1-55673-321-6   PRINTED IN U.S.A.

To our daughter, Karen Grace Kelly,
young elder in a new church
development of her own.

Table Of Contents

Introduction 7

Proper 21 9
Pentecost 19
Ordinary Time 26
    The Dreamer Within You
    Joel 2:23-30

Proper 22 17
Pentecost 20
Ordinary Time 27
    Everything Except God
    Amos 5:6-7, 10-15

Proper 23 25
Pentecost 21
Ordinary Time 28
    How To Hear A Sermon
    Micah 1:2, 2:1-10

Proper 24 33
Pentecost 22
Ordinary Time 29
    When God's "No" Means "Yes"
    Habakkuk 1:1-3; 2:1-4

Proper 25 41
Pentecost 23
Ordinary Time 30
    The Best Offense Is A Good Defense
    Zephaniah 3:1-9

All Saints' Day 49
    Robert Paul, You Were Right
    Daniel 7:1-3, 15-18

Proper 27 57
Pentecost 25
Ordinary Time 32
    Are you Asking The Right Questions?
    Zechariah 7:1-10

Proper 28 65
Pentecost 26
Ordinary Time 33
    Leaping For Joy
    Malachi 4:1-6

Christ The King 73
    No One Comes Into The Kingdom . . .
        Save With Empty Hands
    2 Samuel 5:1-5

Notes 81

A Note Concerning Lectionaries And Calendars 84

All texts in this book are from the series for Lesson One, Common Lectionary. Lutheran and Roman Catholic designations indicate days comparable to Sundays on which Common Lectionary Propers are used.

Introduction

In preparing these sermons I have tried to keep in mind B. Davie Napier's dictum that the "isness" of the Bible is as important as its "wasness."

All the passages, except two, in the lectionary for the last part of the Pentecost season are taken from the so-called Minor Prophets. On the whole, the passages are not as well-known as other selections in the Bible. Nonetheless, I have listened closely in an attempt to capture the "isness" of the prophetic Word for our particular time.

These sermons were preached originally to a newly-organized congregation struggling with its identity and mission. In striving to relate the biblical insights to our contemporary setting I drew upon incidents in the lives of celebrities as diverse as Tom Cruise, Mother Teresa and Sparky Anderson. Observations on more common everyday experiences are included, too.

I will be grateful if these sermons are of some help to pastors who proclaim the Word each Lord's day and to all who seek encouragement in the demanding but exhilarating adventure of faith.

The following people, in one way or another, have contributed to the making of this book. C.S.S. President Wesley T. Runk and Editor Fred Steiner have encouraged me in its preparation. Mrs. Carolyn Henry who typed the final draft of the manuscript always responds to my inquiry, "Can we meet the deadline?" by saying, "Sure, we can!" The members and the friends of Pioneer Presbyterian Church, Belpre, Ohio, were the first to hear the sermons. They are the ones who continually inspire me. Dr. and Mrs. Richard Shipley, Hudson Presbyterian Church, Hudson, Ohio, deserve special recognition. Dick, a new church development pastor par excellence and his wife, Marylin, provided guidance and wisdom at just the right time. Finally, I am grateful to my wife, Arlene. Her love, energy and vision have been incalculable in helping to bring our mission venture to fruition.

Proper 21
Pentecost 19
Ordinary Time 26
Joel 2:23-30

The Dreamer Within You

The setting for the movie *Dead Poet's Society* is a proper New England prep school steeped in tradition and discipline. Into this rather stiff environment comes a new English instructor played by Robin Williams. He has an unorthodox method of teaching. He stands on his desk at times to make a point. He electrifies his students. He has them reading poetry as they practice soccer so that they will see the connection between the two. He prods them to think for themselves, to get in touch with their feelings, to dream their own dreams.

At first, the students are resistant. Everything seems too crazy. Gradually, however, they respond to their teacher's enthusiasm for poetry and life. Soon it becomes apparent that the boys are hungry and thirsty — not for food and drink because most of them come from affluent homes. They are hungry and thirsty for love, for acceptance and for someone to take seriously their personal dreams.

How seriously do we take our own dreams? Are we conscious that we have what Alan McGlashan calls "the dreamer within"? Could it be possible that God is trying to speak to us through our dreams?

The prophet Joel promised ancient Israel that one day "your old men shall dream dreams, and your young men shall see visions (2:28)."

The backdrop for these words was an agricultural crisis. The land had been plagued recently with a swarm of locusts that devastated the crops. Food was scarce. The people were terrified. One day the prophet arrived on the scene to announce that "the day of the Lord" was at hand. This expression signified that God was about to take decisive action in Israel's history.

Joel's prophecy is infused with possibilities about the future. He calls upon his people to rejoice because he has received the promise from God that soon "abundant rain" will come. No longer will they have to contend with "the hopper, the destroyer and the cutter." They will have food to satisfy themselves. Never again will they be put to shame. Their prayers have been answered.

In the teaching of all the prophets "the day of the Lord" had definite implications for the distant future and the end time. Joel introduced his long view with the words: "And it shall come to pass afterward . . ." In the future God will pour out the Spirit upon all people. The sons and daughters of Israel will prophesy. What is more old men shall dream dreams and young men shall see visions. Nor, will such a promise be restricted to just a few people, even "menservants and maidservants" will receive the Spirit." In that day, God will speak directly through the Spirit to each and every one who is open and receptive.

Centuries later, Peter, on the Day of Pentecost appropriates Joel's prophecy of dreams and visions as the text for the first Christian sermon. The prophet's words were fulfilled as God's Spirit like tongues of fire and the rush of a mighty wind came upon the early disciples gathered in Jerusalem. The followers of Jesus who had cowered secretly in fear since their Lord's death, some 50 days previously, now were energized with power, joy and expectation.

The Dreamer within them nudged them out of their comfortable and familiar surroundings in Jerusalem to spread the good news about Jesus throughout Judea, even to the once despised Samaritans, and eventually into the gentile world, in fact to the ends of the earth.

What a dream!

The best news of all is that the same Dreamer is at work within your own life. God is trying to speak to you. Though you may feel spiritually landlocked today, there is something inside you reminding you that you are destined to sail on wider seas.

How shall you respond to God's Spirit, the animating Dreamer within you?

Identify Your Dream

The first task is to identify your dream.

What specifically is God calling you to do? You can be sure that starting out following a dream will not be an easy undertaking.

Chaim Potok in his novel *In the Beginning* tells the story of a Hebrew scholar and teacher who is conscious that the work he does is difficult. It is not painless to motivate students to engage in a disciplined study of the Scriptures. Furthermore, the kind of teaching he does touches the raw nerves of faith and sometimes visibly shakes the students to their core. Consequently, he tells his students: "All beginnings are hard . . . Especially a beginning that you make by yourself. That's the hardest beginning of all."[1]

When my wife and I arrived on the field to gather and to organize our congregation the Mission Committee informed us that we could expect three families in the area to form the nucleus of the new church. That was not many people, we thought, only three families. As it turned out, only one of the three families would actually stay and become a part of the new church development. The situation was more daring that we had realized.

The fact that it rained for seven consecutive Sundays when we began our worship services in a community building did not lift our spirits either. Was the Lord trying to tell us something? What we learned for ourselves was that indeed all beginnings are hard.

Likewise, in identifying our dream it is not always clear just what we are called to be or to do.

Scanning the newspaper the other day I came across the following ad: "Presbyopia — If you are over 40, you've got it."

Presbyopia is the inability of the eyes to focus sharply on things up close, such as small print. The condition comes to us all about the age of 40 and becomes worse as time passes. One of the first signs of presbyopia probably comes when we find ourselves having trouble reading the phone book and other small print.

We all are susceptible to blurred vision when it comes to identifying our dream, too. The meaning of our dream is not always clear at first.

In our new congregation we had little more than a vague idea where our dream would lead us. We had a mere handful of people. Our financial resources were modest. We lacked basic equipment and supplies. We were viewed with suspicion as unwanted competitors by some churches in the area.

Nonetheless, we moved ahead and steadily the dream took shape. We realized that other people in our community were in transition, and we began to appeal to people looking for a new start in life. Some of us were newcomers to the community. Others were beginning new families or were seeking new relationships after suffering brokenness of one kind or another. Still others were simply craving a fresh spiritual adventure.

As we continued our journey we came to believe that the dream was not so much our own dream but God's Spirit dreaming within our fellowship.

Our world needs people who are willing to respond to a compelling dream not only to build new churches but to provide forward-looking leadership in government at all levels, to strengthen our public school system, to wield ecological knowledge and skill to protect our environment. These areas of contemporary society are only a few of the host of challenges awaiting dreamers who are open to the Spirit's leading.

Hold On To Your Dream

After you have identified your dream, the next task is to hold on to your dream.

That objective is not as easy to accomplish as it may seem. Even the most powerful dream can evaporate into thin air with the passing of time.

In my regular walks along the walking trail at the park near the beautiful Ohio River I see in full view the enchanted Blennerhassett Island. The island sits in the middle of the river between Belpre, Ohio, and Parkersburg, West Virginia. I call the island enchanted because of the story associated with the picturesque setting.

One of the most tragic figures of the American Revolution was Aaron Burr. A handsome, slender man from New York state, he showed all kinds of promise. His father was president of the college at Princeton. His mother was the daughter of Jonathan Edwards, the leading theologian in the colonies. He was a patriot and fought valiantly in the war that gained independence from Great Britain. Later he was elected senator from New York, and still later he became Thomas Jefferson's vice president.

But gradually the dream of freedom changed for Burr and self-interest and inordinate ambition took over. He began to have grandiose ideas of invading the Southwest ostensibly to encourage the western states to secede from the Union.

One day he sailed down the Ohio River and came to Blennerhassett Island so named for Harmar and Margaret Blennerhassett who had come from England to build a paradise on the Western frontier. Harmar was wealthy, had a scientific mind, and reflected broad cultural tastes. He also was somewhat eccentric. Burr was able to convince Blennerhassett that his scheme was plausible, and the latter agreed to finance the project. Sometime later, both men were arrested by federal authorities, but Chief Justice John Marshall presided over a trial at Richmond that exonerated both of them of serious crimes.

We probably never will known completely what Burr's motivation was in his Southwest plan. Was it conspiracy or something else less heinous? One thing we do know is that he lost his original dream. It was shattered beyond recovery. His last years were lived as a broken and a disillusioned man.

No matter how promising our dream might be, it is possible to lose sight of it along the way. Since it takes time for a dream to unfold, not everyone has the patience to wait for such developments. Further, if our dream is worth anything at all it is apt to attract opposition. Pressures will be applied against us to deviate from or even abandon the dream. It is not hard to lose the focus of our dream.

Perhaps you have seen on television a rerun of the so-called "Miracle Mile" at Vancouver, British Columbia, in 1954. The Miracle Mile pitted against each other the only two men who at that time had cracked the four-minute barrier. The turning point in the race came near the end of the last lap. Jim Landy of Australia had led all the way, but he wondered during the last lap how close Roger Bannister of England was to him. He turned his head to see, slowed his pace a bit, and in that split second Bannister passed him and never relinquished the lead as he broke the tape.

How essential it is to keep our eye on the target. We must never lose sight of our dream.

Enunciate Your Dream

First, you identify your dream, then you take precautions to hold on to your dreams, and finally, you enunciate your dream.

Mary Jones is pastor of Covenant Church in a small Midwestern community. She realizes that her single congregation does not have an impressive physical plant to attract huge numbers of people. What she does have as pastor is a desire to give her congregation a unique personality. In her case she is looking for people who really want to get involved. If they do not want to, this congregation is not for them. She explains: "When you have vision, people dare to dream the impossible. I believe in trying to get the whole church involved. I am especially drawn to the 'grungies' of society. There is nothing more exciting in ministry than to get people to believe in themselves."[2]

In our own congregation the motif of the pioneer has been at the heart of our dream. Why have we chosen to visualize ourselves in this way? We have an existential reason. We feel like pioneers. We are living on the frontier, not sure of what is coming next. We are willing to take risks. We know deep down inside that we cannot by any means attain our desired objective unless we depend completely upon the grace of God to guide us.

We have a historical reason, too. We live in an area where the first settlements of the Northwest Territory were made. We imbibe the pioneering spirit of the Revolutionary soldiers and their families who left New England to settle Marietta in 1788 and Belpre in 1789. We have inherited a singular legacy.

Most significantly of all, we have a biblical reason. As we study the Bible we confront the pioneer impulse. We notice Abraham and Sarah went out to a far country, not knowing where they are going. The Apostle Paul pioneered too, following the Spirit's dream within him until he not only spread the good news in Asia Minor, but crossed over into Europe and provided the groundwork for the later proclamation of the Gospel by Europeans in the new world of America. And of course, we observed Jesus himself who is fittingly characterized as "the pioneer and perfecter of our faith (Hebrews 12:2)."

In Hannah Green's novel *I Never Promised You A Rose Garden*, a young woman named Deborah struggles with her mental illness. One night she had a dream of winter darkness. Out of this darkness came a great hand, and three pieces of coal were held within the hand. Slowly the hand closed and it became a fist. She could feel the pressure upon the pieces of coal, a crushing sense, almost without relief. After what seemed to be a long, long time the fist relaxed and very slowly opened. She looked to see:

"Three clear and brilliant diamonds, shot with light, lay in the good palm. A deep voice called to her, 'Deborah!' and then gently, 'Deborah, this will be you.' "[3]

Is this not the dream we wish for all people, that they may be changed, that they may start life again, that they may be forgiven, that they have an affirming dream of their own? That message is without question at the heart of the Gospel of our Lord Jesus Christ where we all begin. But in its communication and translation we project our varied emphases, slants and styles that appeal to particular persons and give them hope for tomorrow. Every congregation is summoned to enunciate the dream in one form or another. It is not a once-and-for-all assignment, but a continuing responsibility. We need leaders who will enliven us, interpret and re-interpret our intentions, and keep us moving ahead in a grand adventure of Faith.

Business executive Robert E. Greenleaf in his provocative book, *Servant Leadership,* has a lot to say about goal-setting. He is convinced that the church cannot grow and flourish unless it is caught up in an all-consuming purpose. A growing-edge church constantly looks ahead to the future. In his own words: "Someone in the church must paint the dream. For anything to happen there must be a dream. And for anything great to happen there must be a great dream."[4]

Who is going to paint the dream in your church?

Proper 22
Pentecost 20
Ordinary Time 27
Amos 5:6-7, 10-15

Everything Except God

Robert Coles, a child psychiatrist who taught at Harvard University, decided to travel to the South in the early days of the civil rights struggle to see for himself what effect the tension was having upon little children. He soon developed a special interest in Ruby Bridges, a six-year-old black girl in New Orleans. She walked bravely to class each morning accompanied by federal marshals who protected her from the ever-present abuse of an angry mob.

How was she able to stand such tension? Where did a little girl like Ruby get such courage?

Coles was a trained social scientist. He knew what to look for. He asked her all kinds of questions.

One day, Ruby's mother felt comfortable enough to ask Coles to come to the house. She talked to him at the kitchen table and inquired about what kind of questions he was asking her daughter. He explained that it was important to learn how she was handling stress. He queried her about her appetite, her sleeping habits and other relevant matters.

Ruby's mother replied: "You're a doctor and I shouldn't be asking you questions . . . But my husband and I were talking the other night, and we decided that you asked our daughter about everything except God."

That was the turning point for Coles. When he saw Ruby again he quizzed her from a different angle. Where did she get her courage to face those angry mobs each day? She replied: "I am sure the Lord was watching, not only me but those other people, too." He went and visited her black Baptist Church and learned what gave her courage. The Christian Gospel, the supportive fellowship of a loving congregation, as well as her own family enabled her to be the remarkable young girl she was.[1]

Coles had inquired about everything except God — the most important thing in Ruby's life.

In the fifth chapter of the book of Amos we have an account of the fiery eighth-century prophet addressing his people. The setting is not absolutely certain but in all probability he spoke to them on a feast day at the sacred sanctuary at Bethel. This particular center of worship was the pride of Israel's cultic system. Bethel had everything.

Tradition — Bethel went back to the patriarch Jacob, the spot where he had his dramatic dream of the ladder connecting heaven and earth, with angels ascending and descending upon the ladder. To Jacob, this place was none other than "The House of God," and "The Gate of Heaven." Later Samuel would judge the people in the same place. After King Solomon died and the kingdom was divided, Bethel became one of the chief sanctuaries for the people of Israel.

Sights and sounds — here there was much excitement as animals were killed for sacrifices. Incense was burned. Exhilarating music was played. There was nothing dull about worship at Bethel, in fact there was entertainment for all. The crowds flocked to Bethel.

Prestige — in time Bethel became associated with the king; it was the site of the royal shrine. The best and the most powerful people were apt to be seen at this place.

Yes, Bethel had everything except God.

Amos had been observing the worshipers at Bethel. He noted that they were busy going about their religious duties, but there was the absence of real love and sincere devotion to God in what they were doing. Furthermore, the same people saw no connection between what they were doing at this feast and their dealings in the marketplace throughout the week.

What is riveting about Amos' critique is that the shepherd prophet from Tekoa in Judah did not attack Baalism or foreign idol worship but rather he exposed the emptiness and the hypocrisy of the worship of Yahweh, the God of Israel. God was enthusiastically praised at Bethel, but was conspicuously absent when it came to personal and social relationships at other times and in other places. In a word, Amos was more concerned with a saving knowledge of God and with ethical righteousness as a sign that their religious experience was genuine.

Could it be possible that our worship, habitual as it may be, includes everything except God? We are undoubtedly shocked at such a notion, but the prophet's words ought not to be taken lightly. If we are prone like the Bethel worshipers to glory in entertainment, excitement and ecstasy rather than in an encounter with the true and living God what can we do about it?

Amos has two directives for us.

Seek The Lord And Live

In our Scripture passage today Amos' message contains two basic imperatives. The first one is "Seek the Lord and live (5:6)."

Amos begins with theology. The people have been looking for God in the wrong places. The prophet is emphatic that they should not go to Bethel to find God, but rather they should seek the God of Abraham, Isaac and Jacob, the true and living God.

These words send chills up and down the spine of all who worship. Are we simply going through the motions, or are we really seeking communion with the Lord? It is so natural to deceive ourselves.

For a number of years our new congregation worshiped in an unimposing community building. I recall one particular Sunday when a family came to worship for the first time. The young couple had a little boy who stayed in a kindergarten room in an adjoining building during the morning worship service. After depositing the boy in his room the parents promised to show him the church where the big people worshiped.

When his class was over, the little boy burst into the community building, looked around, and exclaimed to his parents: "Where's the church?" It sure did not look like a church to him. By this time, the worship center had been taken down, the chairs had been put away and what he saw was a group of people standing around eating cookies and drinking coffee or juice. If we had been in the boy's shoes we probably would have said something similar.

It has been helpful for our young congregations not to worship in a regular church building for several years because we have been able to see rather vividly that the church is not a special ecclesiastical-looking structure but rather a group of committed people serving the living Lord no matter where they happen to worship at a given time. We are grateful for the beautiful, functional church building that we now have, but our worship was just as vibrant in our humble quarters when we first heard the call of God to come together as a covenant community of pioneers.

The prophet's words sting us. They penetrate. When we hear them we are obliged to ask ourselves: "What are we seeking? What do we hunger and thirst after? What really turns us on? Is it the true and living God? Or do we just like to be cuddled and to be beguiled while we go through our weekly ritual?"

Surely, something deeply fulfilling should happen when we gather about the pulpit, the font and the table!

William Willimon once asked a Roman Catholic liturgical scholar for some advice on how to stimulate Protestant seminarians to have more appreciation for the Lord's supper. He responded by saying he should begin by teaching cooking classes. Willimon was bewildered. "Because," he explained, "they will never lead the eucharist with conviction until they first learn the joy of giving good food to hungry people."[2]

Something deeply fulfilling does happen in authentic worship. By grace spiritual food is offered. By faith spiritual food is received. Especially in communion we receive the bread of life, and then in Christ's name we go out to feed others.

It you visit Fort Frederica on Saint Simon's Island, Georgia, you may see a historical marker. It commemorates the spot where John and Charles Wesley preached to the Indians in 1736. John Wesley's two-year stay in America was not a happy period in his life, in fact it was for him a time of dashed hopes. If he had died at age 34, he would have been remembered as a good, conscientious man, nonetheless a failure.

After leaving Georgia on Christmas Eve, 1737, John recorded in his journal while at sea: "I came to America to convert the Indians, but, lo who will convert me?"

Shortly after his return to England, on May 24, 1738, to be exact, John Wesley experienced conversion. In his own words: "I felt my heart strangely warmed." He now knew personally something of the vigor in Amos' straightforward appeal: "Seek the Lord and live."

Seek Good And Live

The second basic imperative of Amos' message was "Seek good, and . . . live (5:14)." The first imperative concerned theology; the second one involved ethics. We might add that none of the prophets placed more emphasis upon ethical righteousness than did Amos.

In Amos' day those who worshiped at Bethel held the political, economic and social power in the land; unfortunately, they did not see those persons they oppressed as real people. They knew only that there was money to be earned, rent to be collected, bribes to be made, lavish houses to be built. If anyone stood in their way that was too bad for them.

Do we see the oppressed people of our own day? Or, do we simply ignore them and go about our own religious observances?

Do we see persons who are hurt by racial and religious prejudice?

A recent movie treats this theme with great sensitivity. It is *Driving Miss Daisy* — the story of a Jewish widow living in Atlanta. It is a moving story with lots of humor and light moments. These two people have a difficult time understanding each other and communicating with each other. Eventually, they learn that they have much in common though from radically different backgrounds. Both of them have been subject to prejudice and discrimination. Gradually, they come to see each other in a different light.

What about women? Have we been aware of the oppression that many women have suffered, and some continue to suffer?

In the latter part of the 19th century Donaldina Cameron founded a mission house in San Francisco to help young Chinese women who were brought to this country to be used in the slave trade that flourished at that time on the West Coast. Those men who profited from the slave trade tried everything possible to intimidate Miss Cameron. They threatened her, bombed her home, obstructed her legal battles in court and told the young women themselves that she was nothing more than a "White Witch."

Miss Cameron was not deterred. She stood by her young women, went to court with them as their defender and when they were liberated she provided practical education and training. She is credited with rescuing more than 1,500 Chinese young women from the slave trade. Her concern continues today through Cameron House in Chinatown, as a community center serving families of youth of Chinese and Vietnamese descent. Its programs include domestic violence intervention, youth leadership development and housing advocacy.

Are we aware of the ways we do injustice to our youth?

Young people can be forgotten, too. Year after year a levy to raise funds for the public schools in our community failed. It was voted down by many persons who indicated that they were older and did not have children in school at the present. Consequently, they did not see it as their responsibility to support the school levy now that they were retired and on more limited incomes. The community became divided over the issue.

The Session of our congregation, consisting of the pastor and the elders, finally came to grips with the issue. Eventually, we set forth our own statement backing the proposed levy because we felt it was best for our youth and indirectly for the well-being of the whole community. This was not a carefree public statement to make to our congregation or to the community. As a young congregation we still had a fragile existence. We could not afford to alienate too many people. Our numbers were not that great to begin with. But, it soon became a matter of ethical righteousness. Were we going to seek good or not? Conscious that we were not infallible and could make mistakes, notwithstanding, we felt the situation called for us to take our stand with the children and youth of our community who would suffer the most if we did not have proper funding for education.

We too are called to be peacemakers breaking down barriers that separate people in all spheres of society.

No matter how much we are entertained and are inspired at worship, if we do not translate that liturgical experience into concern for the people about us, many of whom do feel oppressed in one fashion or another, we have missed the point of ethical righteousness. The kind of worship that Amos advocates has a direct impact upon establishing "justice in the gate." The best definition of peace-making that I have run across is these words by Clarence Jordan who starkly delineated peacemaking in these terms: "It's what God does."[3]

On a visit to the dentist a while back I had some time on my hands. I read the *Sports Illustrated* and *National Geographic* magazines. The only other magazines remaining on the table were women's magazines. I picked up one of them (I do not recall which one) and read an article by a woman who was drawing a distinction between infatuation and love. Perhaps thinking of her relationship with a friend she wrote something like the following.

Infatuation is when you think that he is as sexy as Robert Redford, as intelligent as Henry Kissinger, as noble as Ralph Nader, as comical as Woody Allen and as authentic as Jimmy Connors.

Love is when you realize that he is as sexy as Woody Allen, as intelligent as Jimmy Connors, as comical as Ralph Nader, as athletic as Henry Kissinger, and nothing like Robert Redford — but you will take him anyway.

At times, it seems that we do not really have much to do about the way we feel in our deepest personal relationships.

Being a part of dynamic worship is like that, too. We are drawn together not by infatuation with externals, but by sincere love. We have been overcome by an irresistible love. We cannot stay away from the service. We are on the edge of our seats. We know that we are in the presence of the One who is greater than the sum total of the people present.

At the close of the service the living Lord who has called us and bound us together then sends out to "establish justice in the gate," that is in the common round of life not excluding the market place.

Proper 23
Pentecost 21
Ordinary Time 28
Micah 1:2, 2:1-10

How To Hear A Sermon

Walter Cronkite, the former highly-regarded CBS Evening News anchor, is an avid lover of boats. Some years ago, he steered his boat into Central Harbor, Maine. As he approached land he was amazed at the greeting he received. People lined the shore waving their hands at him. He could barely make out what they were saying but their shouts sounded like: "Hello Walter, Hello Walter."

The boat sailed closer and closer to the shore and the crowd, still sending out their greeting to him, grew larger and larger. Shortly after Cronkite tipped his hat in grateful response his boat abruptly jammed aground. As the crowd became quiet he realized what the crowd had been shouting to him: "Low Water, Low Water."

Do we hear only what we want to hear?

How is your hearing today? More to the point, how do you hear a sermon? Could it be possible that we think that we are hearing a sermon when in actual fact we are not hearing it at all.

Our Scripture passage gives us clues on how not to hear a sermon.

Micah did all he could to bid his congregation to hear. He prefaced his sermon with the following pointed words:

> *Hear you peoples, all of you:*
> *hearken, O earth, and all that*
> *is in it   (1:2).*

Micah had considerable gifts. He delivered the Word of the Lord with powerful similes and metaphors. But, he also knew that no matter how eloquent his words if they were not heard all would be in vain.

Some scholars call Micah's prophecy a song, words that might be sung to music like a Medieval troubadour. Other scholars label his prophecy in chapter 2 a "wailing cry" or "a funeral lament."

We must keep in mind that Micah was speaking to important people, rich and powerful landowners and public officials, in the capital city of Jerusalem. He was from the country. His hometown, Moreshath-gath was a rural hamlet, some 25 miles southwest of Jerusalem. When he first came to the city the prophet was appalled by the greed and the corruption that prevailed. He was especially angry with the large landowners who were seeking to buy the property around his hometown, namely the small farms that meant so much to his people. The Word that he had received from the Lord confirmed his own suspicion that what they were doing was not right.

As I read and reread "the wailing cry" of the prophet I said to myself he was a prophet in the mold of our contemporary country singer Willie Nelson. Do not Willie's songs have a wailing sound? Is he not the one who goes around the nation holding free concerts on behalf of the small farmers who have come upon hard times in our day? Maybe you too can capture something of the mood of Micah's prophecy if you can imagine him singing these words in a wailing cry on behalf of the oppressed of his day.

Note some of the specific charges against the large landowners and public officials. He pictured them lying awake at night thinking up schemes to swindle the unsuspecting small farmers. Then, when daybreak came they put their plans into action. Their sin was covetousness. They had enough for themselves already, but they were not satisfied. They wanted more. They coveted houses and fields, the very inheritance of other people. Micah promised that the Lord had set aside a day, not too far off, when what they have done to others will be done to them. Foreigners will come in and plunder their property that they have stolen from others.

The prophet was particularly troubled that women and young children were suffering. Therefore, in the name of the Lord he pronounced "woe" or judgment upon all who did these things.

Also, within the body of our scriptural passage are fascinating words about the reaction to Micah's preaching. His audience did not like his sermon. They called upon him to stop preaching, or, if he must preach, to stick to "religion" and not meddle in political, economic and social matters. Furthermore, they haughtily retorted that they would never be brought to disgrace as he insinuated. In a word, they wanted the prophet to speak soothing, comforting and positive words and eschew irritating, challenging and negative expressions.

Micah was frustrated in that he had a Word from the Lord, but he had no one to hear the Word.

If Micah's audience was a poor example of hearing a sermon, what would be a better model? Are there are few practical ways in which we can hear the Word of the Lord in our own day?

Prepare To Hear The Word

First of all, if we are to hear a sermon, let us come prepared to hear the Word.

George Sheehan, a cardiologist and runner, describes his feelings right before running a race.

"Before I ever park the car, I can feel the adrenalin flowing. The sight of runners warming up sends a rush through my bowels. The smell of the dressing room sets my pulse to racing. The track under my feet makes me break out in a cold sweat."[1]

Do you have similar feelings when you come to worship? Do you have an intense anticipation as the Word of God is about to be read and interpreted from the Scriptures? Are you prepared to hear the Word?

Garrison Keillor of *Prairie Home Companion* radio fame recently published a book titled *We Are Still Married*. He married a woman from Denmark whom he had first met as an exchange student 20 years before at high school. I turned to the back cover of the book with the expectation of seeing a picture of his bride, but there was no picture, not even one of the author. What I found was an essay about a book. Among other things Keillor wrote: "The apostle Paul was not the host of a talk show, or else we'd be worshiping famous people on Sunday mornings; he wrote books, a Christian thing to do. The faith of Jews and Christians rests on God's sacred Word, not on magic or music, and so technology burst forward into publishing . . ."[2]

Yes, Christians are distinctly a people of "the Book." If that is the case should we not be familiar with the contents of the Scriptures? We would not approach another subject or an important assignment of work without adequate preparation, and yet we will come to worship without consulting the primary source of the Christian faith. Would it not be more advisable for us to read the Scriptures throughout the week so that the Book does not seem strange to us when we hear it read on Sunday mornings.

Further, we need not only read the Scriptures but also study them. Numerous small groups, classes and circles within most congregations meet not only on Sunday but during the course of the week to study the Scriptures. One of these groups is just right for you.

Still further, we have the matter of prayer. The Scriptures will remain a closed book until we ask for the guidance of the Holy Spirit to illumine the message for us. Prayer is essential for opening up the meaning of Word of God in the Scriptures to us. Do we approach the hearing of the Scriptures in a prayerful state of mind asking God to be with the one who speaks as well as with the one who hears?

Charles Haddon Spurgeon had extraordinary success as the pastor of his London congregation during the last half of the 19th century. When people would compliment him, he would invariably say that great things were happening in the congregation because he had people who prayed for him. His people came to hear the Word each Sunday with eager anticipation believing that veritably they would hear God's Word addressed to their most pressing needs. How could he not be effective when his praying and expectant people came so well prepared?

Enter Into Dialogue With The Preached Word

Second, if we are to hear a sermon let us also enter into dialogue with the preached Word.

After the worship service one Sunday morning a man greeted the pastor with words to this effect: "We didn't do so well today." The pastor asked what he meant. He continued: "Your sermon was not as helpful as it might have been because I wasn't working with you. There was something in the message that I was resisting."

This man had the right idea about the function of a sermon. Preaching involves not just the person who is speaking but also the whole congregation hearing the message. Both need to be active, not just one person. True preaching is a dialogue with God communicating with the people through those who read, proclaim and hear the Word.

Eugene Peterson asserted: "The Scriptures are a mixed blessing because the moment the words are written they are in danger of losing the living resonance of the spoken word and reduced to something that is looked at, studied, interpreted, but not heard personally."[3] It is only when a word is spoken and heard that we have a true dialogue and the Word of God becomes alive for all concerned.

What is required is that first of all the preacher must hear the Word of God or else he or she will not have reason to speak to others.

Robert Hudnut, a brilliant student at Princeton University, was not certain of his vocation in life at graduation time. Therefore, he decided to explore different possibilities by accepting a Rockefeller Scholarship to study at Union Theological Seminary in New York City for a year to see if the ministry was for him. At this time in his life Hudnut confessed that he never read the Bible any more than the next person. But during the year in Seminary he came in contact with a professor of the Old Testament who gave him a passionate desire to read the Bible. He still remembers a particular chapel service on September 25, 1958, when that professor challenged him by saying: "Go to your Bibles and listen."

Hudnut decided to become a minister, and he has been listening to that Word in the Bible ever since.[4]

Likewise, the people of the congregation must also listen to the Word of God. Such a responsibility implies that people will not remain passive in the presence of the preached Word but will be thinking and feeling along with the speaker about the truth being expounded. There will be a meeting of minds and of hearts. Questions will be stimulated. Personal application will follow. All will be active participants — speakers and hearers alike.

The speaker was not too far off the mark when he began the message with these remarks: "Both of us have a task to perform: I am to speak, and you are to listen. I hope you will not get finished before I do." We are all in it to the end.

In our own young congregation from the very first Sunday we have had lay readers in worship. Such a practice not only gives the lay readers an appreciation for reading the Scriptures, an honor and solemn privilege in itself, but also gives the person an opportunity to do other things, too. I have always encouraged these adults and young people to give the Concerns of the Church including personal comments and an individual witness of their own. Hence, we have experienced the priesthood of all believers. Each Sunday lay readers bring a response to the Word out of the congregation and share with others something of what this dialogical interaction in preaching means to them personally.

Act Upon The Message Received

Finally, if we are to hear a sermon, let us act upon the message received.

David H. C. Read recently retired as pastor of the Madison Avenue Presbyterian Church in New York City after serving for 30 years. In talking to a group of ministers a few years ago he mentioned that he had never yearned to hear the sound of his own voice. But one day he decided to check one of his radio sermons. The night before he set the alarm clock for the right station to come on for the 6:30 a.m. broadcast. What happened the next morning? In Read's own words: "Sure enough I woke to the sound of my own voice — and within a couple of minutes was sound asleep again."[5]

If preachers are apt to go to sleep listening to their own sermons, how much more might we be susceptible to dozing off when the words are not even our own?

Of course, the aim of the sermon is not to put us to sleep, but rather to goad us to action.

Jesus' parable about the sower is a story of how people respond to the Word of God. The seed distributed by the sower is symbolic of the Word. The different kinds of soils represent different human responses to hearing the Word. The best response, according to our Lord, is the soil that was fruitful. The fruit may be a hundredfold or sixtyfold or thirtyfold. The important point is that good hearing results in obedience to the Word and specific action.

In the Letter of James we have the truth put succinctly: "But be doers of the Word, and not hearers only, deceiving yourselves (James 1:22)."

If we have not been transformed in our conduct we have not heard the Word. If we have not reached out in love more after worship than before we have not heard the Word. If we have not left the sanctuary determined to forgive the one who has wronged us, we have not heard the Word.

We approach the hearing of the Word with great anticipation, and leave after receiving the Word resolving to put the

Word into some form of concrete action as we become little Christs to our neighbors.

Tony Campolo tells the story of being invited to speak at a large, affluent church in the Washington, D.C. area. Everything proceeded "decently and in order" with the best in church music and a stately form of worship. Suddenly, a barefoot young man who was slovenly dressed and obviously spaced out on drugs stumbled down the middle aisle. He came to the chancel area and stopped. Everyone was filled with anxiety and suspense. What would he do? Finally, he sat down on the floor just to the right of the pulpit.

The minister proceeded as if nothing had happened, but everyone still felt uneasy. Then, an elderly, well-dressed man got up from his pew and made his way down the aisle toward the young man. He carried with him a walking cane. Some people thought he might try to use the cane to drive the young intruder away. Instead, the old man paused along side the dirty and ragged young man. He sat down with him and put his arm around his shoulder. They appeared to be a strange couple as they sat together in this manner throughout the remainder of the service.[6]

The people heard a real sermon that day. The sermon was dramatically portrayed for them by the two men sitting together on the floor near the pulpit. There could be no mistaking what they were expected to do; it had been shown them even before they had left the service.

Prepare to hear the Word. Enter into dialogue with the preached Word. Act upon the message received. That's how to hear a sermon!

Proper 24
Pentecost 22
Ordinary Time 29
Habakkuk 1:1-3; 2:1-4

When God's "No" Means "Yes"

Augustine in his autobiographical work *Confessions* tells the story of his mother Monica's constant prayers for him. She wished that one day her vagabond son would become a committed Christian. When Augustine decided to leave North Africa and sail for Rome she was horrified. She believed that in Rome's cosmopolitan environment he would go further astray. She pleaded with him not to sail and prayed with tears that God would intervene, but to no avail.

Later, Augustine inscribed these words in the *Confessions* as part of his recollection of the incident: "But thou, taking thy own secret counsel and noting the real point to her desire, did not grant what she was then asking in order to grant to her the thing that she had always been asking."[1]

Sometimes God's "No" means "Yes."

God said, "No" to Monica's immediate petition that her son not sail to Rome in order to respond to "the real point to her desire" namely, her son's conversion. After spending some time in Rome Augustine traveled to Milan where he met Bishop Ambrose who played a key role in Augustine's acceptance of the Christian faith.

The prophet Habakkuk wrestled with a similar dilemma in his own prayers. God had made promises, but they were not yet fulfilled. It was certainly not because Habakkuk had not prayed: "O Lord, how long shall I cry for help, and thou will not hear (1:3)." Habakkuk probably made his complaint to God sometime in the reign of Jehoiakim (609-598 B.C.). As he observed the people of Judah he saw indifference to God's covenant promises, and even more disturbing his people were caught up in endless disputes, legal battles and blatant oppression of the weak and helpless. He was perturbed by the violence that surrounded him on every side.

Habakkuk, weary from praying, wondered if anyone else really cared. Nonetheless, he resolved to be watchful and to wait and see if God would send signs of the imminent fulfillment of the covenant promises. Finally, the Lord answered him and gave him a vision of how he was to act between the giving of the promise and its actual fulfillment.

If you are having trouble discerning the times, if you are finding no answers in your intercessions, if you wonder whether God sees the terrible things that are happening to you and others, then this vision has practical words for you, too.

The prophet's vision contains several guidelines to help your praying.

Learn To Tell Time As God Does

The first guideline in helping you to pray is to learn to tell time as God does.

The movie *Born on the Fourth of July* is based on a true story about a boy who was born on the Fourth of July in the late 1940s. The main thrust of the story focuses upon his experiences as a Marine in Viet Nam and his subsequent disillusionment with the American dream when he returns home. It is an emotional, "gut-wrenching" movie.

One scene early in the movie stands out in my mind. The young man is in high school. He had grown up in a loving middle class family in a small town on Long Island. The family is as American as apple pie. They love the Fourth of July parades. His mother has told him repeatedly he can do anything he sets his mind to. He is a winner. In high school he goes out for the wrestling team and undergoes the most rigorous preparation to make the team. Finally, comes the big match. The local gym is packed to the rafters. He is wrestling in a championship match. His mother, father, brother and sister are all yelling their lungs out. His coach and teammates are cheering for him. The noise is deafening. Everyone knows he will be the champion.

And then, in one quick move, he is pinned. He loses the match. Everyone is stunned. No one can believe it. He has failed. He has let them down. You see the same look on the faces of his family, his coach, his teammates and the fans. Gradually, the camera zooms in on him lying on the floor. The agony of defeat is written on his face. He grimaces but does not move. The sound ceases on the screen. He is alone, defeated, crushed. It seems like this scene lasts for an hour.

Have you ever felt like that in your own life?

Habakkuk did. He saw the signs of defeat and impending doom all around him. He could not understand what was happening. Where was God in all the confusion, chaos and violence? In the first part of Habakkuk's vision the prophet perceives how God calculates time. The Word of the Lord came to him saying: "For still the vision awaits its time; it hastens to the end — it will not lie (2:3a)."

There can be no doubt about it. God's promises will reach fruition but not according to our human timetable but rather according to the divine timeline. If we could really see the larger picture we would not doubt that God is working out an eternal plan.

More to the point, God's eternal purpose "hastens" to the end. I like Elizabeth Achtemeier's comment that this word has the meaning of "pants" — "almost as if God's fulfillment were personified as a runner speeding toward the finish line."[2] In other words, although we may not be aware of it God's eternal purpose is not only moving toward its goal but in point of fact is speeding swiftly and surely toward its destination.

The distinction between different kinds of time in the two Greek words *chronos* and *kairos* is instructive. *Chronos* or chronological time is a time that we are all familiar with. It is measured in seconds, minutes, hours, days, weeks, months, years, decades, centuries and millenia. For some people time passes slowly. They are bored. They are suffering. They are waiting. For other people time passes quickly. They are in love. They are excited about the present moment.

Kairos is another kind of time, essentially a crisis time. It is not measured like chronological time in seconds and minutes but rather it is the time when something new can happen. Just as there is a right time for the farmer to sow his seed, for the business leader to invest in stocks there is a right time for things to happen in the realm of the spirit. In a flash comes an insight; in an unexpected moment we become creative; in the depth of despair a sign of hope is given.

Can we learn like the prophet to begin to tell time like God does and to recognize the difference between mere clock time and crisis time when something really new can take place?

Cultivate The Art Of Waiting

Another guideline in helping you to pray is to cultivate the art of waiting.

In the novel *Zorba, the Greek,* Zorba recalls one morning a time when he had discovered a cocoon in the bark of a tree. He noticed that a butterfly was trying to emerge from the cocoon. He waited a while, but it took so long. Finally, he decided to help the poor creature along. He breathed on the butterfly to warm it, and that act did speed up the process. The butterfly started to come out, but to the horror of Zorba its wings were folded back and crumpled. The butterfly valiantly struggled but could not make it and died. He had forced the butterfly to come out before its time. As he held the little body in his hands he realized the terrible thing that he had done.

Recollecting the event sometime after he said, "We should not hurry, we should not be impatient, but we should confidently obey the eternal rhythm."[3]

Is that not what we all need to do in our own lives — obey the eternal rhythm?

In the second part of Habakkuk's vision the Lord speaks to him: "If it seems slow, wait for it, it will surely come, it will not delay (2:3b)."

Like the prophet we too must learn to wait as God effects the eternal purpose. Admittedly, we have a difficult time being patient in almost everything we do. The Pennsylvania Dutch have a quaint saying: "The more I hurry, the behinder I get." We might not express our impatience in the same way, but we know what the saying means. We are in a hurry, and we often find to our consternation that God is not in a hurry.

As a new congregation we have done our share of waiting. From the very beginning we have been waiting for something: more people to be attracted to our pioneer venture, a site for a new church building, funding to underwrite the costs and the construction of the building itself. The year that it took to constuct the new building seemed like it would never end. The rains came at the beginning of the year and hampered the laying of the foundation and getting the project under roof. The architect, general contractor and building committee often could not agree on basic points. The state government was slow in granting building permits. Suppliers did not send materials on time. One delay after another developed. We wondered if we would ever realize our dream of having our own sacred place for worship.

About six months after the completion of the building the congregation gathered at a family night dinner to review a videotape that had been made during the construction. The video lasted about an hour and a half. We kidded ourselves afterward that an hour and a half was not a long time to build a new church after all. But, what was revealing was we glimpsed the total picture at one setting. Everything seemed to make sense. We could see the end as well as the beginning. Even the delays seemed to fit into the overall picture.

Whatever we may be waiting for God has some assuring words for us. If we would check a good concordance we will find numerous verses in the Scriptures that relate directly to the subject of waiting. If we would like to strengthen our capacity for waiting there is not a more effective practice than meditating regularly upon God's marvelous promises in the

Scriptures. Surely, one of the most cherished promises concerning waiting is the following: ". . . they who wait for the Lord shall renew their strength, they shall mount up with wings like eagles, they shall run and not be weary, they shall walk and not faint (Isaiah 40:31)."

God's Word can help us cultivate the art of waiting.

Live By Faith

Still another guideline in helping you to pray is to live by faith.

Ernie Campbell tells the story of one of the first parades on behalf of women's suffrage held in New York City. It seems that 89 courageous men walked with the women that day in support of their cause. Some time later, after women's suffrage had been made law, another parade was held to mark the triumph. The original small group of men supporters were invited back to share in the celebration. On the day of the parade all 520 of the original 89 men appeared to march in one section.[4]

Anyone can make a pretense of faithfulness when everyone has joined the crusade, but it is quite another thing to step out and be counted when there are only a few. It takes real faith to do that.

The third and final aspect of Habakkuk's vision revealed to him how he was supposed to live until God's promises would be fulfilled. He was to live by faith. Or, in the words of the prophet himself: ". . . the righteous shall live by his faith (2:4b)."

In the intervening time between God's announcement of a promise and the time of fulfillment Habakkuk and his people were to live by faith trusting not in their own strength but in God's acceptance completely. Righteousness implies a right relationship with God. Throughout the Scriptures righteousness is defined not in terms of good works, correct worship or proper pedigree but solely in terms of faith, trust and dependence upon the grace of God.

The Apostle Paul seized upon the prophet's words in explaining the meaning of the Gospel in his communication with the young churches in the gentile world. He wrote: "He who through faith is righteous shall live (Cf. Romans 1:17 and Galatians 3:11)."

After an agonizing spiritual quest Martin Luther rediscovered the same biblical truth and made it the hallmark of the 16th century Reformation Both Paul's faith and Luther's faith were marked by bold risk-taking. They knew when to wait patiently in prayer, but they also knew when being faithful meant direct action no matter what the odds might be against them.

In one of Charles Schultz's cartoons Snoopy is dancing merrily along the way with apparently not a care in the world. Lucy confronts him with the rather dismal words: "You wouldn't be so happy if you knew what was going to happen!" Snoopy ignores her warning and continues to dance merrily on his way and comments to himself: "Maybe it's already happened!"

Snoopy's attitude captures the spirit of all of us who seek to live by faith. We do not have a detailed blueprint for the future, but we are not worried about what is going to happen. The all-important event has already happened in God's decisive saving acts in history, especially in the life, death and resurrection of Jesus Christ. Since that event has happened we can be patient in our praying confident that sometimes God's "No" means "Yes" in the long run. And since that event has happened we can be alert for those creative and renewing moments of *kairos* when God wants us to take risks and become participants by faith in something really new.

Proper 25
Pentecost 23
Ordinary Time 30
Zephaniah 3:1-9

The Best Offense Is A Good Defense

Reading the title you may jump to the conclusion that I do not know football. To be sure, the saying usually goes: "The best defense is a good offense."

But consider the plight of Joe Paterno when he became head coach of the Penn State Nittany Lions in 1967. He realized that he did not have a squad of outstanding athletes, particularly defensive players. To Paterno, defense was the key to winning football games. What was he to do? In his own words: "I had to find a way of playing great defense without great defensive athletes."

Therefore, he spent the summer before the season began diagramming hundreds of defensive plans until he hit upon the idea of adding an extra defensive lineman to stop the opponent's option play in which the quarterback pitches the ball to a halfback or fakes and keeps the ball and runs himself. By adding an extra man to the defensive line, however, this meant that he had only three men in the backfield to guard against the pass. Hence, he devised a zone system whereby the three men would shift to whichever side of the field the ball was thrown.

Paterno went on to win more than 200 victories, including two national championships, in his years as head coach at Penn State. He not only proved his theories about the value of a great defense, but also demonstrated that he was teachable and was flexible, a man willing to correct an unsatisfactory situation when he confronted one.[1]

Zephaniah, the prophet, had a problem, too. The people to whom he spoke in the city of Jerusalem did not see the need to correct anything. Such an attitude would lead to their downfall. Listen to the prophet's cry on behalf of his beloved city:

"She listens to no voice, she accepts no correction. She does not trust in the Lord, she does not draw near to her God (3:2)."

That his people could act in this manner was beyond the comprehension of the prophet. After all God had done for them, how could they be so indifferent?

God had given them the law of the covenant grounded in divine mercy to lead them in their personal and social conduct. But this holy law had been violated not only by the people but by their leaders — officals, judges, priests and even prophets.

Further, God had disclosed providential care in the laws of nature. Each morning and each evening follow with consistency showing that there is order and purpose behind the universe.

Still further, God had intervened on behalf of Judah in her relationship with other seemingly invincible nations. Had the people forgotten the judgment that had come upon other nations, a judgment that would undubitably come upon them if they persisted in their oppressive and uncaring ways?

Zephaniah heard a gracious God sigh: "Surely she will fear me, she will accept correction," but such was not to be; the prophet sadly observed: "But all the more they were eager to make their deeds corrupt (3:7)."

There is not much that can be done now. The covenant people will have to wait for a later day when the Lord will begin again. In that day people will truly call upon the name of the Lord.

How is it with us today? Are we willing to be corrected by God's Spirit as we listen to the Scriptures? Are we teachable? Are we willing to accept self-discipline?

In our new congregation we soon learned that not everyone was able to "hack it." Some people would be curious about our new enterprise of faith. They caught something of the spiritual adventure involved, but after a short time it soon became evident that much of the new church development was not glamorous but rather was a mix of hard work, self-discipline and continuing sacrifice. Not everyone who first showed interest was able to accept these conditions, and they eventually dropped out.

What does happen when we are willing to let God correct and teach us? What are some of the dominant features of disciplined people?

Disciplined People Are Liberated

First of all, disciplined people are liberated.

"Where is Nolan Ryan?" the reporters asked. He had just pitched a no-hit game (Monday, June 11, 1990). At 43 he was the oldest major league pitcher to throw a no-hitter. Besides being the all-time strike out pitcher in major league baseball, it was nothing new for him to pitch a no-hitter, this one was the sixth of his career.

Now the game was over. The reporters flooded the Texas Rangers' clubhouse to interview the hero of the hour. They found him in the middle of the clubhouse riding his stationary bicycle. He explained to them: "You don't deviate from your routine."

People, like Nolan Ryan, who take discipline seriously, do not have the sense of being enslaved but rather they have the sense of being liberated. The underlying purpose of discipline is to set us free.

Water that is undisciplined, free to wander wherever it wishes, ends in a swamp. Water that is disciplined, hedged in on each side by strong banks, becomes a mighty river that flows toward a certain destination. Likewise, our lives without structure become swampy and ineffective.

Richard Foster helps us to visualise what positive discipline is by drawing a picture of a narrow ledge with a sheer drop-off on either side. The chasm on the right side is a way of life marked by human striving after righteousness, the teaching of moralism. The chasm on the left side is a way characterized by the absence of human striving, the teaching of antinomianism, that is there is no law. On the ledge itself is the path of discipline that leads to transformation, healing and freedom. To this vivid picture Forest adds the caveat: "We must always remember that the path does not produce the change; it only puts us in the place where the change can occur. This is the way of disciplined grace."[2]

While affirming discipline as liberation we might add a footnote of our own, namely that genuinely disciplined people also have a sense of humor and are willing to give and take.

Winston Churchill once received an invitation to attend the opening performance of George Bernard Shaw's play *Pgymalion*. Shaw wired him: "Am reserving two tickets for you for my premiere. Come and bring a friend — if you have one." Churchill wired back: "Impossible to be present for the first performance. Will attend the second — if there is one."

Disciplined people follow a path with persistence but they also have their moments of lighthearted detachment from life that can be liberating, too.

Disciplined People Are Flexible

Second, disciplined people are flexible.

Leo Buscaglia readily concedes that his college students become frustrated with him when he changes his mind. "When my students raise their hands, and say, 'That isn't what you said Tuesday.' I say, 'I know. I've grown since Tuesday. Do you expect me to be last Tuesday's Leo today?' "[3]

Disciplined people may have strong convictions and be willing to express them, but they also have the capacity to modify these convictions if they receive new truth.

Many of us have had to grapple with rigid thinking. Probably for many of us the practice goes back to childhood. Once we had made up our mind on something we did not like to change it. In fact, we might have feared changing it. New evidence that threatened to undermine our cherished ideas was unsettling. Far better for us to remain in our original thought patterns than to venture forth into the uncertain and often painful task of revising our ideas. We often reason that at least we can manage our small and restricted world.

On the other hand, disciplined people realize that learning is a lifetime occupation. We are never through learning something new. We undoubtedly would prefer if everything stayed the same, but we soon come to fathom that change is a constant in life. The world around us changes, and we must not be afraid to incorporate into our own world and life view changes that will enrich our own adventure of faith.

In our day when the Christian life often is depicted in soft, sentimental and simplistic terms it is refreshing to reread John Bunyan's remarkable allegory, *Pilgrim's Progress.* In his imaginative story Christian meets friends, such as Faithful and Hopeful, but he also encounters Worldly Wiseman, Hypocrisy and Giant Despair. Christian is never certain what might be around the next corner — Vanity Fair or the Slough of Despond. He must be adaptable and resilient. In the end, despite all adversities, God's Spirit enables him to overcome and enter the Celestial City.

A short time ago I heard Bernie Siegel give a lecture to about 500 people. Dr. Siegel is the New Haven, Connecticut, surgeon who has helped many people afflicted with cancer with his emphasis upon faith, love and hope. During the course of the lecture he told the story of a teenager named Susan who moved to a new house, and her mother insisted that she do volunteer work during the summer. She went to the local nursing home where she was asked to read to a Mr. Johnson. She went to his room and introduced herself. She asked him how he was. His reply was "I'm all right so far."

She wondered what he meant by that expression. He proceeded to tell her a story. "I'm like the man who falls out of a window at the top of a 30-story building. Each floor he goes by, people lean out and say, 'How are you?' And the man replies, 'I'm all right so far.' "

Siegel tells his cancer patients and others he works with that the attitude of saying "I'm all right so far" can get you through a lot of things. Such an attitude is an open rather than a closed view of life that is bound to have a salutary effect not only on our physical health but on our whole being.

Disciplined people are flexible.

Disciplined People Are Creative

Finally, disciplined people are creative.

In 1890 a Canadian named James Naismith was faced with a career decision as he neared the completion of his senior year as a Presbyterian theological student in Montreal. Was he to seek a pastorate upon graduation or was he to follow what he was coming to suspect was the prompting of God's Spirit to seek a Christian calling in the field of athletics?

Shocking not a few of his professors, Naismith resolved his dilemma by choosing the latter course. He enrolled in a recently-opened Y.M.C.A. training school in Springfield, Massachusetts, now called Springfield College. The school combined an emphasis upon both spiritual and physical development. Naismith was a superior athlete in soccer, lacrosse and other team sports. Soon after going to the school as a student who had already completed seven years of higher education, he was appointed to the faculty of this pioneer institution in teaching physical education.

One day Luther Glick, the president of the college, gave Naismith an unwanted assignment. Naismith was charged with teaching a winter term class of rebellious students who hated the endless calisthenics associated with the class. Glick hinted that the young instructor might create a new game that the students could play during the long New England winter.

Naismith was a disciplined person, and he went about his task in systematic fashion. First, he tried to adapt children's games for adult use but the students only mocked his efforts. Next, he experimented with outdoor adult sports and sought to apply them to an indoor setting but these efforts proved to be unsatisfactory, too. Finally, he decided, if possible, to invent an entirely new game. He had in mind a game less violent than the ones he was accustomed to playing, one that would require team spirit and new skills. He drew up a simple set of 13 rules which he posted on the bulletin board. Then, to the astonishment of his students, he proceeded to nail two peach baskets at either end of the Springfield gym. He had his players, nine on either side, dressed in long, gray trousers and short-sleeved jerseys, line up to play the first basketball game ever in December, 1891.[4]

Disciplined people have been led to make creative contributions not only in the realm of sports but in all aspects of life. They may not know at first just where God is leading them, but their discipline keeps them plodding along until the inventive movement comes.

Science fiction writer Ray Bradbury in a recent book on writing has a great deal to say about the value of discipline for the creative person. He observes that behind the remarkable artistic achievements of Leonardo da Vinci and Michelangelo were thousands and thousands of unknown sketches. He calls our attention to the surgeon who before he operates on a human being in a critical condition has dissected and redissected thousands of tissues and organs preparing himself for the crucial moment. Bradbury sums up his point in these words: "eventually quantity will make for quality."[5]

The quantity of those endless sketches and dissections is what makes for the quality of the masterpieces of portraits and landscapes and the precise skill of the surgeon under fire.

Our nation was founded by disciplined people. The pilgrims were a people whose lives were captive to the Scriptures. In 1620 when they left England they did not sail directly to the new world. Instead, they went to Holland to say goodbye to colleagues who had fled there in an earlier day of persecution. John Robinson, their pastor, preached a sermon to them before they set sail in the Mayflower for America. Among other things he said: "The Lord hath more light yet to break forth out of his Holy Word."

It is not surprising therefore that people who received such a charge would be open to creative possibilities with regard to church and state on the other side of the Atlantic. They firmly believed God's providence had led them to their own errand in the wilderness. We are profoundly indebted to these disciplined and creative men and women in their own day.

God would like to liberate us, too. God would like us to be flexible and open individuals. God would like us to become the creative people we were designed to be.

Are we willing to be corrected? Are we willing to be disciplined for the glory of God?

All Saints' Day
Daniel 7:1-3, 15-18

Robert Paul, You Were Right!

Professor Robert Paul and his family had just returned to Hartford Seminary from a trip to the Rocky Mountains. As a doctoral student in church history studying with him I had always been stimulated by his lectures and seminars. Now, I was anxious to talk with him and with his gracious and perceptive wife, Eunice, to get their impressions of the trip.

Paul, a native of England, was ecstatic about the natural beauty of America, but he also was appalled by the lack of appreciation for what he called "a sense of being rooted in history." Most American Christians live in the present, and long for the future, he contended, but they have little recollection of the past. In his own England he was constantly reminded of the past with its plethora of Medieval churches and cathedrals, ancient Roman ruins and other historical architecture.

After receiving his doctorate from Oxford University Paul served for a number of years as a minister of a Congregational Church in Leatherhead. Later, he became Associate Director of the Bossey Institute in Geneva, Switzerland. Still later, he pursued a distinguished teaching and writing career in church history at Hartford, Pittsburgh and Austin seminaries.

I am profoundly indebted to this extraordinary human being who deepened my love of church history. He made the English and New England Puritans (his specialty) come alive. Furthermore, he expanded my vision of the world-wide church in our own time.

How do you observe life today? Like many American Christians do you tend to live in the present and future tenses and tend to neglect the past tense? Do you think something really old means a pop tune from the 1960s? Would you side with Henry Ford who is alleged to have said: "History is bunk"?

If you answer "Yes" to the above questions, then today's theme on All Saints' Sunday in the church calendar may be just right for you. This special day in the liturgical cycle is designed to give us historical perspective, to help us remember unique persons who have lived in earlier days but who can and do still influence our own lives in the present.

Our Old Testament passage centers on a dream of Daniel during the reign of Belshazzar, king of Babylon. In the night vision Daniel saw four distinctly different kinds of beasts coming out of the sea. He was alarmed by his strange vision and sought interpretation. He was told that the four beasts symbolized four oppressive kings who would threaten the faithful. Daniel was not to fear, however: ". . . the saints of the Most High shall receive the kingdom and possess the kingdom for ever, for ever and ever (7:18)."

The saints or faithful ones are given a promise that eventually they will overcome. At any given moment the verdict might not be clear; in fact, quite often it seems that the powers of evil are so potent that they will never be defeated. But, daily observation of events is only a limited perspective. The whole of history is needed in order to correctly view difficult times. The saints' kingdom is not a transient one but one which is everlasting. Those people who are committed to the Most High will ultimately overcome.

Now, what do the saints of the Most High have to do with us today as we pursue our own journey of faith?

The Saints Give Us Examples

First, our journey of faith is enriched because the saints give us examples.

The magic of the Olympic Games provides an analogy to help us understand the example of the saints. If we have not actually been present at the Olympics, we probably have seen the spectacle via television. What is it about the opening ceremonies that excites us so much?

The huge stadium, frequently seating 100,000 or more people?

The stirring entrance of the athletes representing the nations of the world?

The music, the speeches, the drama?

For me, the high point of the pageantry is when a runner enters the stadium carrying a torch that has been transported to this particular place from Olympia, Greece, the origin of the Games. Conveyed across national borders, sometimes spawning the oceans, the torch signifies the relationship between the current Olympics and those Games that have gone on before. The runner ascends the steps, lights the flame and the Games officially begin.

The athletes participating in the Games are connected to a glorious past that goes all the way back to the first Games held in Olympia. As they engage in their contests they are keenly aware of what Robert Paul has called "a sense of being rooted in history."

The New Testament writer in the Letter to the Hebrews seems to have in mind the Olympics or some other significant athletic event when he writes the following words:

> *Therefore, since we are surrounded by so great a cloud of witnesses, let us also lay aside every weight, and sin which clings so closely, and let us run with perseverance the race that is set before us, looking to Jesus the pioneer and perfecter of our faith, who for the joy that was set before him endured the cross, despising the shame, and is seated at the right hand of God.*   Hebrews 12:1-2

Like Daniel who appealed to the saints of the Most High, to cheer up those who were suffering persecution, the writer to the Hebrews appeals to the "cloud of witnesses" to fortify Christian exiles who faced opposition from the powerful Roman state. They are exhorted to run their own race of faith spurred on by their vital connection with the faithful of the past.

But do we really feel comfortable having the saints looking over our shoulder as we attempt to run our own race of faith? Are not these exemplary women and men in a class by themselves?

Charles Schulz captures our fears in one of his cartoons. Lucy is trying to develop a close relationship with Schroeder, but his idol Beethoven keeps getting in the way. In the first scene Lucy is leaning on the piano while Schroeder plays. She asks: "Schroeder, why is it you like Beethoven better than you like me?" Finally, after some hesitation Schroeder replies: "Beethoven was Beethoven, and you are you." After thinking for a few moments, Lucy retorts: "That doesn't even leave room for discussion."

When we compare ourselves with the saints we may wonder whether there is any room for discussion. Even a casual glance at the Scriptures should allay our fears. The great heroes and heroines of faith were not plaster saints. They were real flesh-and-blood people who made mistakes, and in some instances, they committed shocking sins. Abraham, the father of Israel, when his life was threatened was not above passing off his wife as his sister to protect himself. David, "a man after God's own heart," sinned flagrantly and had to be reprimanded by the prophet Nathan.

The reason that these people are examples is not because they point to themselves as paragons of virtue, but rather because they direct our attention to God's faithfulness. They are singular examples of what God's grace was able to do in and through them despite their human frailities.

All Saints' Sunday has special relevance for our young congregation. We know something of the thrill of risk-taking living on the cutting-edge of the church's frontier. We would not be completely honest, however, if we did not admit that now and then we bemoan our paucity of local traditions.

As we listen to the Word of God spoken to us about the saints of the Most High something happens. We begin to realize that even an infant church has roots and is associated with a grand heritage.

Was it not our own denomination, part of the larger church, that commissioned and organized us in this mission work? We are not an isolated unit, but we are a new cell in the larger body.

Further, do we not have sisters and brothers of faith in every country in the world? Young and small as we are we are still a part of the universal Christian church.

Still further, are not the saints of all the ages our ancestors, too?

May we not claim the following as our own?

Twentieth century witnesses — Mother Teresa, Alexander Solzhenitsyn, Bishop Tutu, Dietrich Bonhoeffer, and Kagawa;

Social reformers — William Booth, Elizabeth Fry and Walter Rauschenbusch;

Pioneer missionaries — William Carey, Mary Slessor and David Livingstone;

Puritans — Thomas Hooker, John Cotton and Thomas Shepard;

Reformers — Martin Luther, John Calvin, Thomas Cranmer and Menno Simons;

Medieval saints — Thomas Aquinas and Francis of Assisi;

Church fathers — Ignatius, Irenaeus and Augustine;

Jesus, the Twelve and Paul;

Daniel, the Prophets, Moses and Abraham and Sarah.

These people are our saints, too. They steer us to the faithfulness of God. They lead us away from our own little world and fix our attention on the eternal promises of God.

The Saints Give Us Encouragement

Second, our journey of faith is enriched because the saints do not only give us examples, but they also give us encouragement.

On All Saints' Sunday we rehearse the stories of faithful people in order to be inspired. Because they were overcomers in the midst of adversity, we believe that we also can overcome our own trials in our own time and place. Because they did it, we can do it, too.

Who are the saints who encourage us? We have called to mind stalwart witnesses out of the distant past, but do we not have saints who affect us for good in the recent past, too? Do we have saints as close to us as in our own family history?

I have always been a fond admirer of the actor Jimmy Stewart. Reading an article in the newspaper I learned something about him I had not known before. In an interview Jimmy was telling the reporter about his return to Hollywood after serving as a pilot in the Air Force during World War II. He had a little house in Brentwood, and one day his family came from Pennsylvania to visit him. During the conversation with his family his dad asked him, "Where do you go to church?" Jimmy began to make excuses that he was busy and besides he indicated that the church was too far away. Later in the day, his father said he was going for a walk. In about an hour he returned bringing with him four men.

Jimmy's father said, "Son, you didn't look far enough when looking for a church. There's a church two blocks down the road. It just hasn't been built yet. These four men are elders of the church. I told them that you'd be glad to help the church get started."[1]

And Jimmy Stewart did help them. The church became his own, and later the church took on special meaning for him when he and his wife were married there.

His father had eyes to see something that the son could not see. He knew there must be a church nearby, and his faith led to find one, even though the building itself had not yet been constructed for the new congregation. How fortunate are we if we have someone in our family who helps us to see in similar fashion.

On the other hand, the saints who encourage us might be total strangers.

A Hallmark Hall of Fame television movie titled *My Name is Bill W.* tells the story of Bill Wilson and Dr. Bob Smith, the founders of AA, Alcoholics Anonymous. A chance meeting of these two individuals in Akron, Ohio, sparked one of the century's most amazing renewal groups.

In the last scenes of the movie Bill Wilson, now retired, travels with his wife on their way to a new home to California. They decide to stop in Iowa to attend an AA meeting that happens to meet in the local church. No one recognizes him as the founder of AA, but he is accepted warmly. He introduced himself: "My name is Bill W." How thrilled he is as he sits back and watches the group in action. They listen to each other, care for each other and all call upon a Higher Power at work in their lives. When Wilson leaves the meeting he has confirmation once again that his idea is working. Within a context of anonymity and confidentiality people are bearing witness and giving hope to one another.

Could a baseball manager be a saint, too? Tommy Lasorda has been called many names, but he probably has never been called "a saint."

Orel Hershiser, a young man with a strong Christian commitment, was having a difficult time during his rookie season as a pitcher for the Los Angeles Dodgers. Used primarily as a relief pitcher, he could not seem to pitch effectively. One day, early in the month of May, he was summoned to the manager's office. He feared what might be coming. More than likely he would get the word that he was being sent back to the minor leagues.

Lasorda came right to the point and reminded him of the mistakes he had made in recent games. Then, moving closer to him, and shouting louder and louder he said to him: "Do you know what your problem is? You are scared to pitch in the big leagues." The manager went on to say that he thought that Orel had the making of a big league pitcher; in fact, he implied that if he had his stuff he would be in the Hall of Fame today. Lasorda closed the animated conversation by declaring that starting today he was going to give his young pitcher a new name "Bulldog," and he wanted him to believe that he was the best pitcher in baseball.

Knowing that his manager had faith in him turned things around for Hershiser and he went on to become one of the premier pitchers in major league baseball. He now calls his blunt-speaking manager: "a true motivator, encourager, cheerleader."[2]

We all need someone who will help us feel good about ourselves. Fortunately, God has a way of sending that select person to us at the right time.

Ira Progoff through his intensive journal workshops has taught people how to get in touch with their past by using a journal. He makes much of what he calls "stepping stones" — significant points of movement along the path of life. He explains: "We go back into the past by means of the stepping stones in order to reconnect ourselves with the movement of our personal lifetime, and so that we can move more adequately into our future."[3]

We can recover the stepping stones in a variety of ways, but one of the most advantageous ways is to recall specific persons who have influenced our lives at various junctures along the way.

Who are the persons who have intersected your life at a given moment and shifted you in a new direction?

A parent? A teacher? A pastor? A coach? An author? A stranger? A friend? An enemy? Who was the person for you?

When you return home after worship today spend a quiet time reviewing your own history and the people who have helped you along your own spiritual journey to this day. Express your gratitude to God for each one of them. If possible, speak to them or write them a letter telling them how much they have meant to you. These are "the saints" of the Most High" who have exceptional meaning for you.

Thank you, Robert Paul, you were right. We all do require "a sense of being rooted in history" if we are to be God's faithful people. Because of the examples of the saints we are encouraged to make our own witness in the confidence that God's grace will move in and through our lives, too.

Proper 27
Pentecost 25
Ordinary Time 32
Zechariah 7:1-10

Are You Asking The Right Questions?

An article titled *Widespread Spiritual Hunger Should Be Major News Story* caught my eye on the editorial page of the Sunday paper. The author, Bill Tammeus, a columnist for the *Kansas City Star*, speculated about some journalists and some scientists who refused to see truths that are not physical. The case in point was Pope John Paul II's visit to Mexico. Huge crowds appeared wherever he spoke. In San Juan los Lagos an estimated one million people gathered in a meadow to listen to him.

Why did these enormous crowds seek out this man? Such questions were never addressed by most news stories which covered the papal visit.

'Tammeus asks: "Why are they so interested in a man who can only give them sermons, not jobs, food or shelter?"[1]

The prophet Zechariah confronted a similar situation. On December 7, 528 B.C., he received a delegation from the sanctuary town of Bethel. The people represented some of the returning Jews from the Babylonian Exile. Sharezer and Regemmelech were the leaders. Scholars are not agreed on the identification of Regemmelech. (The name literally means "Friend of the king.") He may have been a Persian convert to Judaism.

In any event, Zecharish is queried about whether or not they should continue to maintain the quarterly fast that was instituted to remind the Jews of the destruction of the temple in Jerusalem in 587 B.C. Should they continue to observe the fast even though the new temple was being re-constructed?

The Word of the Lord came to the prophet with a question for the people. During the past 70 years when you fasted, "was it for me that you fasted (7:5)?"

In other words, what was your motivation in fasting? Was it merely a sentimental observance, an exercise in self-pity? Or, was it a genuine fast concentrated upon the Lord of hosts and the true purpose behind the fast? Did the people really know why the temple had been destroyed? Had they any idea how God had been offended by their lack of devotion, their blindness to poor, hurting and neglected people in their midst?

Zechariah, like Amos and Micah, called for ethical righteousness. More important than a ritual fast that had lost its original intent was the charge to render true judgments, to show kindness and mercy, to refrain from oppressing weaker persons and not to devise evil in their hearts (7:8-10).

What about our own day? Are we asking the right questions? Are we really absorbed in the nature and function of our religious devotion and worship, or are we like the Bethel delegation caught up in the self-centeredness of things that do not really matter?

In our young congregation we have had to re-examine our motives from the start of our existence. In a new church development the pressure is tremendous to ask survival questions rather than to ask mission questions. It seems so natural to entreat: "How are we going to attract new members?" "Where is the money coming from?" "How soon will we be able to build?"

More demanding questions that should be raised are the following: "Why has God called us to start this project in the first place?" "What can we learn about the Gospel in our new beginnings with forced simplicity and meager resources?" "Who are the people in distress on our own doorstep and beyond?"

All too often people unite with a church because they want something from such membership — peace of mind, a feeling of togetherness and promises of future prosperity. How much better it is to challenge people not to ask what their church can do for them but rather what can they do for their church. All new members in our congregation are asked to complete a volunteer form indicating in what capacity they will serve. The underlying assumption is that we all have gifts in helping to build up the body of Christ and to extend its outreach.

What are some of the specific questions we should be raising regarding prayer and corporate worship?

How Shall We Adore Our Lord?

The first question we might ask is "How shall we adore our Lord?"

One of Jean Francois Millet's most well-known paintings is *The Angelus*. The poignant scene shows a peasant farmer and his wife stopping work for a moment out in the field. As the bells announce the Angelus they bow their heads in prayer. The weariness of work subsides as they adore their Lord in silence.

We all require a quiet time during the day for nothing else but the adoration of God. For some the best time may be early in the morning before the frantic pace of the day overwhelms us. For others the close of the day when the world prepares for sleep is the ideal time. For still others it may be noon or some other stopping-off-place during the course of the day that serves their lifestyle best.

No particular time is sacred in itself. The crucial point is that adoration becomes central in our living. Adoration is the beginning of worship and prayer. Before we ask anything, whether it be for others or for ourselves, even before we confess our sins, we praise God plainly for being God. We stand in awe in the presence of the Almighty.

What Sins Should We Confess?

A second question we might ask is "What sins should we confess?"

In Susan Howatch's novel, *Glittering Images,* Charles Ashworth, an Anglican clergyman and scholar, suffers a spiritual collapse. He seeks help from Abbot Jon Darrow who is known as a skilled and an understanding counselor. The abbot soon realizes as they talk that while others see only the "glittering image" projected by this highly successful man deep inside is a clearly troubled soul weighed down with excessive baggage of guilt and of regrets. Gradually the abbot persuades Ashworth to unload the unnecessary baggage he is carrying. But, he can only go so far: "My function is simply to offer you the chance to get rid of any bags which you don't want to carry any more, but the decision to keep or discard each bag must be yours and yours alone."[2]

Confession of sin is essential to our spiritual wellbeing. We cannot be the vibrant people we want to be until we find liberation from the burdens that press upon us. In our inner being we know that something is out of alignment with God's intended will for us. Certainly, God knows that we are unworthy, even before we make our personal confession. Healing begins when we are willing to face our true selves, and when we are ready to have something done about the oppressive loads we carry.

We are not fully cleansed until we hear the word of God's forgiveness speaking to us. Then, we resolve by God's grace not to repeat the sins of the past and to face tomorrow with humility and gratitude. To confess our sins and to receive God's pardon is like being released from a darkened room and walking in the light once again.

How Inclusive Should Our Petitions Be?

A third question we might ask is "How inclusive should our petitions be?"

Of course, we are urged to pray for our basic needs; nevertheless, a major part of our petitions ought to be for others.

Another famous painting with a spiritual message is Albrecht Durer's *Praying Hands*. Durer, a contemporary of Martin Luther in 16th century Germany, was a poor art student when he found a friend who opened up new possibilities for him. His friend, also a promising art student, said he would work in a kitchen and serve meals to raise money so that Durer could continue his vocation. When Durer's art began to sell, then his friend agreed that he would return to his own first love.

Eventually Durer's attractive wood carvings did sell, and it was time for his friend to resume work as an artist. However, the manual labor had so stiffened his hands that no longer was he able to exhibit the skill he once possessed.

One day as Durer returned home earlier than expected he discovered his friend praying quietly with folded hands. He was well aware that he could not give his friend back the use of his hands, but he did want to do something to repay him for his great sacrifice. Finally, he decided he would paint these praying hands so that the world would be reminded of all those who sacrificially pray and work for others.

Is there any higher calling than intercessory prayer? Throughout the world there are people in all walks of life, not just in monastic orders, who devote themselves to praying for others. These intercessors are not usually in the limelight, but their influence for good upon others must be of inestimable value in God's sight.

We engage in intercessions for a variety of reasons. First and foremost, we pray for others because we believe God loves them and wants us to pray on their behalf. Although intercession is a mystery in the ultimate sense, the Scriptures are consistent in stating that God works through human beings like ourselves to work out the eternal design.

Second, we make intercessions because we know that when we do other people are changed. Today, we accept the fact that through television words, music and pictures are sent to all parts of the world. Can we also not believe on a higher level that God has provided a network of cooperation whereby our loved ones can be influenced and changed for the better?

Third, we intercede because such prayers also do something for us. We cannot sincerely pray for some one else without a change taking place in our own life. Our horizons are lifted. We begin to see others as God sees them. Furthermore, we begin to act in assisting those for whom we are praying. In other words, we decide to become part of the answer.

Whom Should We Serve?

A final question we might ask is "Whom should we serve?"

Adoration, confession and petitions will seem shallow unless they issue forth in some kind of service. Not only the prophet Zechariah, but all the prophets underscore ethical righteousness as the logical outcome of genuine prayer and worship.

Dr. Karl Menninger's funeral service was held on July 21, 1990, at the First Presbyterian Church in Topeka, Kansas, where he had worshiped throughout his adult life. The pastor giving the eulogy for this 96-year-old man cited his extraordinary contributions to American psychiatry that brought this discipline out of the "snake pit" era into a new day where real hope was offered to the mentally ill.

The pastor also recollected the first year of his present pastorate in 1984. At the time, Dr. Menninger was 91. The pastor and a youth group during the Christmas season went to the shut-in families of the congregation including the Menninger home to sing carols. "But Dr. Karl was not home that evening," the pastor said, "He was having Christmas with the prisoners at the county jail."[3]

Do we see the lonely, hurting, neglected people around us? They are in our neighborhood. They work alongside us. We meet them in our social contacts. They are in the nearby nursing home. Yes, as Menninger knew well, they are especially in our prisons.

In many Christian worship services people pass the peace of Christ to one another at some point in the service. It is a dramatic symbol of shared love, but it does little good unless the same love also flows out beyond worship to encompass friends and strangers alike in our Monday to Saturday existence.

James Herriot, the Yorkshire, England veterinary surgeon, who has written many popular books, such as *All Creatures Great and Small* and numerous other books, was interviewed one day by a Canadian reporter. The man rather cynically asked Herriot if he would be skipping off one day to a tax haven to avoid the crushing British taxes on his book royalties. The author assured the reporter he had no desire to leave the Yorkshire dales. He had all he ever wanted — wonderful people, soccer, cricket, tennis, rugby — what else would he ever need?

At the conclusion of the article the reporter made this statement: "The man and the writer seem nicely consonant one with the other."

What a fine tribute!

Is that not what Zechariah was driving at in his appeal to his people? Did he not want their profession and their practice to be "nicely consonant one with the other"? Is that not what we want, too?

We can make a telling start right now in our prayers and in our worship — if we ask ourselves the right questions.

Proper 28
Pentecost 26
Ordinary Time 33
Malachi 4:1-6

Leaping For Joy

The scene was the Connecticut House of Representatives in Hartford. The date was May 19, 1780. About noon the skies began to darken and by midafternoon the sky was pitch black. Many people were struck with fear believing Judgment Day had come. Some of the representatives fell to their knees begging God to avert this catastrophe; others called for an immediate adjournment. Colonel Davenport, the Speaker of the House, rose to his feet and stated: "The Day of Judgment is either approaching or it is not. If it is not, there is no cause for adjournment. If it is, I choose to be found doing my duty. I wish, therefore, that candles may be brought."[1]

How would you respond to the announcement that the end of the world had come? Would "the Day of Judgment" strike fear in your own heart?

Not a few so-called prophetic teachers of the Bible make a living out of feeding on fear of the end time. How tempting it is for prognosticators to pretend to know the exact date and to know the key figures involved when the day of the Lord will come. All my life I have heard predictions that the particular decade in which I happened to be living would be the one when Christ would return. The antichrist was supposed to be Hitler, then he was supposed to be Stalin. He became whomever the latest, most powerful dictator might be. Every time predictions of precise dates and the identification of specific personalities associated with the second coming have to be revised. Jesus stated explicitly that no one knows when all of these "last things" will take place, not even him, only the Father (Matthew 24:36)." Despite that clear warning some people are still gullible and trust certain prophetic teachers to have esoteric knowledge that no one else possesses. They really are convinced that someone has the key that will unlock the mystery of the ages.

One of our church members handed me several sheets of paper that he said were attached to the front door of the church building. The pages consist of a series of disjointed Scripture quotations with the predominant theme of God's impending judgment. The papers do not contain the scriptural emphasis upon God's grace, peace and forgiveness.

Who would write such words? Perhaps they were written by someone who sincerely does believe the end of the world is at hand, or they were written by a discontented person who has soured on life. We will probably never know.

Might the one who placed those papers on the church door be someone who thought our young congregation was not taking our work seriously enough? What with all the times of fellowship and refreshment after worship, covered dish dinners and little and big parties here and there it could seem to someone that all we do is have a good time. I am not convinced that partying is a bad thing. After all, we have labored, struggled and sacrificed in order to see our new church take shape. It has been good for all of us to take time off periodically to laugh, to feast and to enjoy each other's company.

Such thoughts bring us to our scriptural passage for the day in the book of Malachi. The prophet is speaking to his people who have become discouraged. They have begun to question the wisdom that other people who ignore or violate the law of Moses seem to prosper. Should they not soften their consciences and follow suit?

Malachi declares the word of the Lord admonishing his people to continue in their faithfulness to the law of Moses. The day of the Lord is coming. That great day will be preceded by the appearance of Elijah who personifies all true prophets in Israel. Furthermore, the day of the Lord will bring the conquest of evil and the triumph of God's people who remain bound both to the law and the prophets.

Employing the imagery of the sun Malachi sees all those who have followed evil being burned up like stubble. The faithful, on the other hand, will receive from the same sun "with healing in its wings" wholeness and salvation. Malachi's words are consistent with the main points of Hebrew prophecy regarding the end time.

The prophet also includes another enlightening image in his summary. I was struck by the vibrancy of the following words: ". . . you shall go forth leaping like calves from the stall (Malachi 4:2b)."

For those who believe the day of the Lord will be like calves, which having spent the night in their stalls, at daybreak go leaping about joyfully in the sunlight. Such will be the joy of the faithful in that day. The prophet's exhortation to leap for joy is an even better response to "the Day of Judgment" than Colonel Davenport's desire to do his duty.

Consider what practical implications for the journey of faith this fascinating simile suggests.

Leaping For Joy Implies Celebration

First of all, leaping for joy implies celebration.

The note of celebration is sounded throughout the pages of the Scriptures. As we have just noticed, Malachi, the last book of the Old Testament, ends with celebration, like calves bursting forth from their stalls at daybreak. The book of Revelation, the last book of the New Testament, also ends with celebration, like the marriage supper of the Lamb.

In between, celebrations of one kind or another abound. Jesus in one of his parables tells of a man who accidentally stumbled upon a treasure while plowing in a field. Overcome with joy he goes and sells all that he has to buy that field. Jesus tells another parable about a merchant who searches the world for the pearl of great price. Once he finds it, he sells all that he has to purchase that one pearl. The kingdom of heaven is like that; it is worth abandoning everything else in order to obtain it.

If celebration is going to be characteristic of the great day of the Lord in the future, should we not be learning how to celebrate here and now?

When C. S. Lewis came to write his autobiography he titled it *Surprised by Joy*. How else could he explain what happened to him? God reached this skeptical Oxford University professor one day while he was riding a bus. He was so startled by the awareness of God's loving presence that he could only describe the intervention by saying he was "surprised by joy." Henceforth, he devoted the rest of his life to being "an apostle to the skeptics" seeking to convince disbelieving intellectuals that the Gospel was indeed a treasure of celebration.

Many people who enter the kingdom testify to the party-like atmosphere. Following the Lord is not drudgery. There is no room for long faces in the company of the redeemed. Despite its clear-cut demands Christian discipleship is deeply satisfying. There is a direct link between obedience and joy. We begin in obedience and end in joy. No one has more of a claim on celebration than the one who has been stirred by God's amazing grace.

Even though the celebrative mood has a solid scriptural base, how often the upbeat, life-affirming person is suspect. One of my favorite Lincoln anecdotes is about the two Quaker ladies who were talking about the two leaders in the Civil War. The one woman insisted that Jefferson Davis and his cause would win. When challenged by the other woman to explain why, she said: "Because Jefferson Davis is a praying man." The other replied: "Abraham Lincoln is a praying man, too." "Yes," retorted the first woman, "but the Lord will think Abraham is joking."

There was something about Lincoln's carefree, almost irreverent, manner that made many people question his sincerity. Lincoln, however, was a compassionate man who not only could laugh at others but could laugh at himself, too.

If we are to know something of the joy of the kingdom we must find out how to celebrate.

Leaping For Joy Implies Play

Second, leaping for joy not only implies celebration but it also implies play.

Surely, the calves in Malachi's striking image were not only celebrating their release from the long night in their stalls, but also they undoubtedly lost little time in frolicking about with the exuberance of sheer play.

If there is going to be play in that great day of the Lord in the future, should we not be cultivating the art of play here and now.

Sparky Anderson is one of the best major league baseball managers of all time. He manged the Cincinnati Reds ("The Big Red Machine") during their glory days in the 1970s and currently manages the Detroit Tigers. He is the only major league manager in history to win a World Series in both the National and the American Leagues. How does he approach his job? He contends that anyone who sees managing as a job is in the wrong business. In his own words: "This is not a job. This is fun."[2]

What would an Olympic swimmer say about Sparky's boundless enthusiasm? Betsy Mitchell from Marietta, Ohio, has won gold medals in the 1984 Olympics, the 1990 Goodwill Games and in other competition. She presently holds the American record for the 100 meter backstroke swimming event. Her mother started her swimming at an early age. By the time she was nine or 10 years old she was beginning to show signs of being a good swimmer. Her Marietta YMCA coach observed, however, that at that time many people thought Betsy fooled around too much. She did not take her sport seriously enough. On the other hand, perhaps it was her playful attitude toward swimming that actually made it possible for her later to become a champion swimmer.

Not just major league baseball managers and Olympic swimmers view life in terms of play, but other supposedly serious-minded people do, too. For instance, Annie Dillard, the perceptive essayist and nature writer, tells of doing research on a book during a summer at Hollins College in Roanoke, Virginia. Tired of reading one afternoon, she gazed out the library window and caught sight of a softball game in progress. Since she just happened to have her fielder's glove with her, she went to see if she could join the game. As it turned out, the ball players were part of a music camp being held at the college for two weeks. She soon determined that the boys were musical wizards, but they were atrocious softball players. But, she did enjoy their jaunty banter. "All right Macdonald," they jeered when one kid came to bat, "that pizzicato won't help you now." Dillard said she played with them every day, but she was always terrified that she "would bust a prodigy's finger on a throw to first or the plate."[3]

Whoever we are — a manager, an athlete, a writer or someone else — we need to learn how to play and not take life too seriously. What is play for you? Golf? Snorkeling? Walking? Running? Mountain climbing? Gardening? We all require some kind of diversion to give us a balanced life, and even more, to prepare us for playing in that great Day of the Lord.

Leaping For Joy Implies Adventure

Leaping for joy not only implies celebration and play but it also implies adventure.

The leaping calves in Malachi's delightful figure of speech suggest also that the calves were ready to explore their surroundings and to see what the new day might bring.

If that is the case in the future, should we not be looking for adventure in our lives here and how?

The Day of the Lord is not the end but rather the beginning of a fresh phase of our faith pilgrimage. Paul Tournier concludes his book, *The Adventure of Living*, by describing the life beyond life as "a new departure, a leap into a new adventure."[4]

Yes, leaping for joy embraces "a leap into a new adventure."

We are called to be pilgrims. Let us not get too settled in the place where we are. Octogenarian Malcom Muggeridge anticipates the future by exclaiming: ". . . the world itself only becomes the dear and habitable dwelling place it is when we who inhabit it know we are migrants, due when the time comes to fly away to other more commodious skies."[5]

What a waste of time to be always speculating about the tantalizing details associated with the end time. David Redding in his book, *God Is Up To Something,* sums up the crucial matter "Hope thrives on the suspense of God's next visit, whether or not it is his last."

Are we ready to meet God in the next visit around the corner? God's daily surprises are only a foretaste of what we will encounter some day. To live with a spirit of adventure now is to know in advance something of the ultimate joy which will be ours in that day.

An American woman while touring in Mexico one morning met a boy selling oranges. She thought to herself that an orange would be just the right thing to quench her thirst. Having compassion on the boy, she offered to buy the remaining six oranges he had left. The boy would only sell her three.

"Why won't you sell me the other three?" she asked.

"What will I do in the afternoon?" he replied.[6]

The boy might not have been shrewd financially, but he did know something about the meaning of life. It is important that we have something to do in the afternoon.

You may be near mid-life. I say to you: What are you going to do in the afternoon? What are you going to do with the second half of your life? Will you be bored? Will you simply mark time? Will you dissipate your energies in aimlessness? What will you do with the second half of your life?

Malachi speaking the word of the Lord bids us to envision living out our days leaping for joy. Celebrating, playing, adventuring — that is the way to prepare ourselves for the lifestyle that will prevail in that day.

Christ The King
2 Samuel 5:1-5

No One Enters The Kingdom . . . Save With Empty Hands

The black man standing in the arena was an affront to Der Fuehrer's authority. The scene was the 1936 Olympic Games held in Berlin, Germany. The black man was Jesse Owens of The Ohio State University representing the U.S.A. He was aptly called "the fastest human alive." Der Fuehrer was Chancellor Adolph Hitler who had recently risen to power championing an arrogant theory that his "Aryan race" of "supermen" would conquer the world. In implementing his theory he began systematically to stamp out the Jews in a bitter expression of prejudice and discrimination. Hitler also publicly denounced Blacks, Negroes as they were called then, as an inferior race. Jesse Owens, in his estimation, should not even be present at the Games.

Jesse Owens was not only present, but he went on to win four gold medals in the 100-meter-dash, the 200-meter-dash, the broad jump and the 400-meter relay race. He demolished Hitler's claim that the Aryan race was superior to all others. Furthermore, this soft-spoken black athlete embarrassed Hitler and undermined his pompous authority in the heart of the Fatherland.

Today is Christ the King Sunday in the liturgical calendar, an appropriate time for us to grapple with the whole question of authority. We may not be in danger of being seduced by an evil power such as Hitler, but we may not be clear on the authority to whom we give allegiance.

In 2 Samuel 5:1-5 we have a glimpse into the historic occasion when David and the elders of the tribes of Israel entered into a solemn covenant. By this time David already was recognized as king in Judah, but now he sought to bring Israel and Judah into a strong United Kingdom serving the Lord. On that day the representatives of the people agreed to submit themselves to the authority of King David and sealed their vow with a covenant.

When David became king of the United Kingdom of Israel and Judah he began a line of succession that lasted for more than 400 years. It was from David's line that the Jewish people later expected a Messiah. No one is hallowed more than David in the Hebrew tradition. Despite his human failings, he is still considered the ideal king.

Christians have high regard for David, too, but we tend to see David in relationship to "a greater David," namely Jesus Christ. One day Madeleine L'Engle was shown a color photograph of an icon, probably from Armenia which pictured King David in a sitting position. In one hand David held a harp, and in the other hand he was holding a child sitting on his knee. The caption under the picture read: *King David with Christ on his lap.*[1]

We believe that the living Christ spans the centuries. The child on David's lap in this picture is in actual fact his Lord. Did not Jesus suggest just this point in his debate with the Pharisees when he asked them about the Messiah, "Whose son is he?" When they replied that he was the son of David, Jesus quoted the Psalms showing David calling the Messiah "Lord." Jesus then raised the further question: "If David thus calls him Lord, how is he his son (Matthew 22:45)?" Christ and David are forever linked together, but Christ was to teach and to demonstrate in his own life a fresh understanding of kingship.

As the Pentecost season draws to a close we are confronted with the all-important question of authority. Let us ask ourselves a few questions about this urgent matter.

Who Has Authority Over Us?

The first question to ask is "Who has authority over us?"

I will never forget a worship service held during the first year when our congregation was being gathered. We were not yet officially organized as a church. We asked people who desired to be a part of this new congregation to sign the charter. After the sermon people were invited to come forward to sign the charter on the table. The names on this petition requested Presbytery to organize us as a new church.

At the heart of the charter was a covenant which read as follows: "We promise and covenant to live together in unity and to work together in ministry as disciples of Jesus Christ, bound to him and to one another as a part of the body of Christ . . . ."

Watching scores of people come forward and make their commitment to Christ and to this new congregation sent shivers up and down my spine. What a moving scene. For some people it was the first time that they had ever made a personal commitment to Jesus Christ as Lord. For other people the decision meant leaving an already established congregation with all its entitlements and striking out on an uncertain journey. Not a few agonizing decisions were made that day.

The underlying issue in signing the charter was one of authority. Who was going to rule over us? We chose to bind ourselves together in a covenant under the kingship of Christ.

Such an act of submission has continuing implications for all aspects of our life together. In our confession of faith we must be careful that our own special formulation of words and thoughts do not become sacrosanct to the extent that we cannot confess our faith in any other manner. If this happens, our creed is treasured more than the Lord we profess to serve.

In our worship service we bear witness to the victory and power of God in Christ by means of a liturgy which may be simple or complex. The crucial point is whether the liturgy becomes an end in itself or whether it is viewed as a means that can be adapted and renewed. In a word, is our particular liturgy or Christ the lord of worship?

In our form of government we provide a structure that is indispensable to the ordering of the Christian community.

But it is possible to manipulate our structure in such a way as to deny the kingship of Christ.

Another way of looking at the locus of Christian authority is to consider the following three-fold distinction. The church's message is the spoken Word of God prized because it is the means by which we first heard the good news about Christ. Nevertheless, the spoken Word carries with it the possibility of faulty communication and misinterpretation.

Hence, we have an even higher regard for the Scriptures, the written Word of God. These 66 books constitute the primary source document of the Christian faith. Without the Scriptures we would not know about God's great plan of redemption in Christ.

Finally the Scriptures lead us to Christ, the living Word of God. He is the full and the perfect expression of God. He is the one to whom the Scriptures bear witness. Christ the King is our supreme authority.

What Kind Of Authority Is It?

Once we have determined who has authority over us, we must proceed to ask: "What kind of authority is it?"

When the Soviet dictator Stalin was told of papal disapproval of his oppressive policies against his own country, he was purported sarcastically to have replied: "How many divisions does the pope have?"

All too often we tend to equate authority with political clout and military might. Over against this popular view consider Peter Marshall's story about the keeper of the spring. He was a man who lived high in the Alps above a certain Austrian town. He had been hired by the town council to clear away the debris from the pools of water up in the mountain that fed the beautiful spring that flowed through the town. Since the man did his work so well the village prospered. Graceful swans floated in the spring. The surrounding countryside was irrigated. Several mills used the water for power. Restaurants flourished for townspeople and for a growing number of tourists.

Years went by. One evening at the town council meeting someone questioned the sum of money paid the keeper of the spring. No one seemed to know who he was, or even if he was still on the job high up in the mountains. Before the evening was over, the council decided to dispense with the old man's services.

Weeks went by and nothing seemed to change. Once autumn came, however, the trees began to shed their leaves. Branches broke off and fell into the pools high up in the mountains. Down below the villagers began to notice the water had become darker in color. A foul odor appeared. Swans were not around anymore. The tourists had left, too. Soon disease spread through the town.

When the town council reassembled they realized to their chagrin that they had made a costly mistake. They found the old keeper of the springs and hired him on the spot. Within a few weeks the spring cleared up, and life returned to this Alpine village as they had known it before.[2]

The story of the keeper of the spring comes closer to Jesus' concept of authority. Though standing in the Davidic tradition, Jesus re-cast the notion of kingship into the image of the servant. To exercise real power in Jesus' kingdom is to serve others. Such power is greater than political clout or military might. Paradoxically, though it may seem, there is power in weakness. Those persons who submit themselves to the way of servanthood soon learn the truth of their Lord's words.

We are never closer to the meaning of genuine authority than when we gather at the communion table. As we hear the words: "This cup is the new covenant in my blood (1 Corinthians 11:25)" we are face to face with the king who is a suffering servant. Our Lord not only tells us what to do, but he shows us how to do it in his supreme sacrifice of love for us. The kind of authority Jesus taught and lived was embodied in the image of the servant.

How Submissive Are We To Authority?

First we ask, "Who has authority over us?" Next, we ask, "What kind of authority is it?" Finally, we ask "How submissive are we to authority?"

We say that Christ the King reigns over us, but does he? Or, are we encumbered with so many other commitments that our professed central allegiance is mitigated.

Gail Ricciuti was requested to give the commencement address when she was graduated at Princeton Seminary. She challenged the graduates "To Live as if a Sojourner." Instead of degrees she bestowed on them knapsacks. She was concerned that they might be carrying too much luggage, theological and otherwise, with them as they left to serve Christ. In contrast to suitcases, knapsacks were light, more suitable for Christ's sojourners.

Riciutti asks: "And have you ever tried to hug someone with suitcases in your hands?" She answers her own question by stating: "With the heavy baggage of a densely-packed static theological system, you might give those you are called to love twisted sacroiliacs, or worse — lame them for life."[3]

This is good advice, not only for graduating theological students but for all Christian sojourners. We have been called to travel lightly. We are on a journey of faith. None of us has arrived. We may remember a thrilling moment of decision when we first responded to the awakening of God's love for us. But, we cannot live in the past no matter how nostalgic that moment might be for us. Our present task is daily surrender, a constant re-commitment of our lives. We never know in advance where submission to the kingship of Christ will lead us.

Are we over-burdened today? Do other commitments, legitimate as they may be, crowd out our paramount commitment to Christ? Are we holding back something from our Lord that should be surrendered?

Andrew Greeley, a Roman Catholic priest, sociologist, prolific writer and recently a best-selling novelist, one day returned to his former parish in suburban Chicago for a celebration. At the close of his message he told the following legend about King Fergus of the Kingdom of Kerry in the West of Ireland. I share the story in abbreviated form. Fergus was a good and wise king, but eventually he grew old. Realizing he was soon to die he summoned all his loved ones around to bid them farewell. He loved his people, and he loved the green hills, blue sky, golden fields and silver lakes of his Kingdom of Kerry. Hence, before he commended his soul to God he scooped up a clump of thick, rich Kerry turf in his right hand.

In a short time the king was standing at the gates of the eternal city facing Saint Peter. Introducing himself, he asked to enter the city — all the time clutching the clump of Kerry turf behind his back. Peter punched the computer and learned that the king had a good record indeed. He was about to let the king in when he spied his clutched hand. When interrogated, the king reluctantly admitted that he had a wee bit of Kerry turf to remind him of his home. Peter informed him forthrightly that it was against the rules: "No one enters the kingdom of heaven, save with empty hands."

King Fergus was insistent that he be permitted to enter the gates. He would not part with his clump of Kerry turf. Even when the Lord himself came out to explain the rules, the king would not budge. Each time he was told: "No one enters the kingdom of heaven, save with empty hands."

After much time went by, finally King Fergus decided the rules were not going to be changed for him. He threw down his clump of Kerry turf and approached Peter again. This time Peter punched the escape code, and the big gates opened wide. And what do you think the king found inside?

"Inside, waiting for King Fergus . . . was . . . The green hills and blue skies and the golden fields and the silver lakes and the whole kingdom of Kerry!"[4]

Whatever we are holding back is so small and so insignificant in contrast to the grand gift the Lord wants to give us. Let us surrender whatever we are clutching to ourselves and accept what Christ the King has to offer us.

"No one enters the kingdom . . . save with empty hands."

Notes

The Dreamer Within You
1. Chaim Potok, *In the Beginning* (New York: Alfred A. Knopf, 1975), p. 3.
2. Donald P. Smith, *Congregations Alive* (Philadelphia: The Westminster Press, 1981), pp. 39-40.
3. Harriet Green, *I Never Promised You A Rose Garden* (New York: Holt, Rinehart and Winston, 1964), pp. 242-243.
4. Robert K. Greenleaf, *Servant Leadership: A Journey into the Nature of Legitimate Power and Greatness* (New York: Paulist Press, 1977), p. 88.

Everything Except God
1. Robert Coles, *Harvard Diary: Reflections on the Sacred and the Secular* (New York: Crossroad, 1988), pp. 135-136.
2. William Willimon, *Sunday Dinner* (Nashville: The Upper Room, 1981), p. 60.
3. Clarence Jordan, *Sermon on the Mount* (Valley Forge, PA.: Judson Press, 1970), p. 34.

How To Hear A Sermon
1. George Sheehan, *Running & Being: The Total Experience* (New York: Simon and Schuster, 1978), p. 163.
2. Garrison Keillor, *We Are Still Married: Stories and Letters* (New York: Viking, 1989), back cover.
3. Eugene Peterson, *Reversed Thunder: The Revelation of John & the Praying Imagination* (San Francisco: Harper & Row Publishers, 1988), p. 12.
4. Robert Hudnut, *Arousing the Sleeping Giant* (New York: Harper & Row, Publishers, 1973), p. 43.
5. David H. C. Read, "Eutychus — or the Perils of Preaching," *The Princeton Seminary Bulletin*, Vol. VI, No. 3, p. 168.
6. Tony Campolo, *Who Switched the Price Tags?* (Dallas: Word Publishing, 1986), pp. 174-175.

When God's "No" Means "Yes"
1. Augustine, *Confessions and Enchiridion,* translated and edited by Albert C. Outler (Philadelphia: the Westminster Press, 1955), p. 105.
2. Elizabeth Achtemeier, *Nahum-Malachi, Interpretation* (Atlanta: John Knox Press, 1986), p. 43.

3. Nikos Kazantzakis, *Zorba the Greek* (New York: Simon & Schuster, 1959), pp. 120-121.
4. Ernest Campbell, *Locked In A Room With Open Doors* (Waco, Texas: Word Books, Publisher, 1974), p. 115.

The Best Offense Is A Good Defense
1. Joe Paterno with Bernard Asbell, *Paterno: By the Book* (New York: Random House, 1989), pp. 96-101.
2. Richard Foster, *Celebration of Discipline: The Path to Spiritual Growth* (San Francisco: Harper & Row, Publishers, 1978), p. 7.
3. Leo Buscaglia, *Living, Loving & Learning* (New York: Fawcett Columbine, 1982), p. 164.
4. Bernice Larson Webb, *The Basketball Man* (Lawrence, Kansas: The University Press of Kansas, 1973), p. 54ff.
5. Ray Bradbury, *Zen in the Art of Writing: Essays on Creativity* (Santa Barbara, CA: Capra Press, 1989), pp. 122-123.

Robert Paul, You Were Right
1. Marian Christy, "Jimmy Stewart: 81 Years of Family, Working Hard," *The Boston Globe,* appeared in *The Columbus Dispatch*/Sunday, Nov. 26, 1989, p. 10G.
2. Orel Hershiser, with Jerry B. Jenkins, *Out of the Blue* (Brentwood, Tennessee: Wolgemuth & Hyatt, Publishers, Inc. 1989), p. 13.
3. Ira Progoff, *At A Journal Workshop* (New York: Dialogue House Library, 1975), p. 103.

Are You Asking The Right Questions?
1. Bill Tammeus, "Widespread Spiritual Hunger Should Be Major News Story," *The Kansas City Star,* quoted on the Op. Ed. page of *The Columbus Dispatch* (Ohio), June 3, 1990.
3. Susan Howatch, *Glittering Images* (New York: Alfred A. Knopf, 1987), p. 223.
3. "Psychiatry's Dr. Menninger Is Eulogized," Topeka, Kansas (AP), *Parkersburg News* (WV), Obituary Page, July 22, 1990.

Leaping For Joy
1. Quoted in Gerald Kennedy, *A Reader's Notebook* (New York: Harper & Brothers, 1953), p. 90.
2. Sparky Anderson with Dan Ewald, *Sparky!* (New York: Prentice Hall Press, 1990), p. 109.
3. Annie Dillard, *The Writing Life* (New York: Harper & Row, Publishers, 1989), pp. 28-29.

4. Paul Tournier, *The Adventure of Living* translated by Edwin Hudson (New York: Harper & Row, Publishers, 1965), p. 243.
5. Malcom Muggeridge, *Chronicles of Wasted Time, I: The Green Stick* (New York: William Morrow & Company, Inc., 1973), p. 18.
6. Edward Fischer, *Life in the Afternoon: Good Ways of Growing Older* (New York: Paulist Press, 1987), p. 1.

No One Enters The Kingdom . . . Save With Empty Hands
1. Madeleine L'Engle, *A Stone For A Pillow* (Wheaton, Illinois: Harold Shaw Publishers, 1986), p. 201.
2. Catherine Marshall, *Mr. Jones, Meet the Master* (New York: Fleming H. Revell Company, 1951), pp. 147-148.
3. Gail A. Ricciuti, "To Live as if a Sojourner," *The Princeton Seminary Bulletin,* Vol. IV, New Series, 1983, No. 1, p. 6.
4. Andrew Greeley, *Confessions of a Parish Priest: An Autobiography* (New York: Simon and Schuster, 1986), pp. 502-507.

A Note Concerning Lectionaries And Calendars

The following index will aid the user of this book in matching the correct Sunday with the appropriate text during Pentecost. All texts in this book are from the series for Lesson One, Common Lectionary. Lutheran and Roman Catholic designations indicate days comparable to Sundays on which Common Lectionary Propers are used.

(Fixed dates do not pertain to Lutheran Lectionary)

Fixed Date Lectionaries *Common and Roman Catholic*	**Lutheran Lectionary** *Lutheran*
The Day of Pentecost	The Day of Pentecost
The Holy Trinity	The Holy Trinity
May 29-June 4 — Proper 4, Ordinary Time 9	Pentecost 2
June 5-11 — Proper 5, Ordinary Time 10	Pentecost 3
June 12-18 — Proper 6, Ordinary Time 11	Pentecost 4
June 19-25 — Proper 7, Ordinary Time 12	Pentecost 5
June 26-July 2 — Proper 8, Ordinary Time 13	Pentecost 6
July 3-9 — Proper 9, Ordinary Time 14	Pentecost 7
July 10-16 — Proper 10, Ordinary Time 15	Pentecost 8
July 17-23 — Proper 11, Ordinary Time 16	Pentecost 9
July 24-30 — Proper 12, Ordinary Time 17	Pentecost 10
July 31-Aug. 6 — Proper 13, Ordinary Time 18	Pentecost 11
Aug. 7-13 — Proper 14, Ordinary Time 19	Pentecost 12
Aug. 14-20 — Proper 15, Ordinary Time 20	Pentecost 13
Aug. 21-27 — Proper 16, Ordinary Time 21	Pentecost 14
Aug. 28-Sept. 3 — Proper 17, Ordinary Time 22	Pentecost 15
Sept. 4-10 — Proper 18, Ordinary Time 23	Pentecost 16
Sept. 11-17 — Proper 19, Ordinary Time 24	Pentecost 17

Sept. 18-24 — Proper 20, Ordinary Time 25	Pentecost 18
Sept. 25-Oct. 1 — Proper 21, Ordinary Time 26	Pentecost 19
Oct. 2-8 — Proper 22, Ordinary Time 27	Pentecost 20
Oct. 9-15 — Proper 23, Ordinary Time 28	Pentecost 21
Oct. 16-22 — Proper 24, Ordinary Time 29	Pentecost 22
Oct. 23-29 — Proper 25, Ordinary Time 30	Pentecost 23
Oct. 30-Nov. 5 — Proper 26, Ordinary Time 31	Pentecost 24
Nov. 6-12 — Proper 27, Ordinary Time 32	Pentecost 25
Nov. 13-19 — Proper 28, Ordinary Time 33	Pentecost 26 Pentecost 27
Nov. 20-26 — Christ the King	Christ the King

Reformation Day (or last Sunday in October) is October 31 (Common, Lutheran)

All Saints' Day (or first Sunday in November) is November 1 (Common, Lutheran, Roman Catholic)

www.ingramcontent.com/pod-product-compliance
Lightning Source LLC
Chambersburg PA
CBHW060850050426
42453CB00008B/927